Out Of The Shadows

Tanya Michelle
xx

Tanya Michelle is a self-publishing author from

Alberta. Her work can be found at

WWW.TANYAMICHELLELIFESTYLE.CA

Publishing/ all other inquiries may be sent to

tanyamichellelifestyles@gmail.com

ISBN-13: 978-1727174861

ISBN-10: 1727174860

cast all
YOUR ANXIETY
ON HIM BECAUSE
HE CARES
FOR YOU.
1 PETER 5:7

-For My Daughters-

Understand that it took All of this to be All that i am now. I have no regrets and hold no grudges. My hope is that you Love and Honor yourself as well as each other always. And know that You are Loved, You are Worthy, You are meant for more!!

Contents

Throughout the pages of this book, I have shared stories that I have kept in the shadows for close to two decades.

Every single one of us have a story and some of us have more secrets hidden amongst our story than others. In most cases, we allow the world to see only a fraction of who we really are. We allow the world to see is the highlight reel of our lives. It's edited, it's rarely Raw and Real! It's even more difficult now with social media and all the wonderful posts and pictures of all of these people living their best lives. . It's very rare that people are ever vulnerable enough to share their most private moments, biggest mistakes and fears. Do we really let people know us?

To those who question why I wrote this book and how can I share such horrific, painful, traumatic experiences of my life? The answer is actually simple and only really became clear this past year. You see, I share a daughter with my Pimp. And as she matures and builds a family of her own, I see so much of me, in her. She like so many of us, struggling with her worth and unfortunately was raised by a man that unknown to her, left scars to last a lifetime.

We are actually a family of women now. Twenty years later and I am a mom to four beautiful, talented, amazing human beings, ages 21,18, 16, 12 and I need them to know their worth. I need them to understand all those times that we would have discussions about boys and they would get frustrated and think, I was just being a mom. Keeping this secret is keeping me hidden in my shame. Breaking my silence is for me and my girls, choosing to never be a voiceless victim again. I may have escaped my pimp but the shame of my story has haunted me for almost twenty years. Well not anymore! I'm taking my life back, stopping the chatter of others judgment as well as my own negative self-talk! Today I let that all go and give my shame to God.

I have done my best to express my thoughts and feelings as accurately as I can when talking about people, places, and events that took place during that horrible time in my life. I have reconstructed these scenes and conversations from my memory to the best of my ability: they truly describe my thoughts, feelings, and behaviors in those moments.

Writing this did not happen from front to back. It was a process and I had to dump ten years of memories and then sort through and decide what needed to go in for you all, the reader, to truly understand the epidemic that is Human Trafficking. For the most part, I have used Real first names, but where I can't remember them, I have used Pseudonyms.

I have thought very hard about how to portray everyone in this book and have tried to treat the tougher scenes with dignity, grace, compassion, and honesty.

Above all, I hope this book gives a deeper understanding as to what is happening around the globe to young victims of Human Trafficking and the damage it leaves on our souls after we escape! What I experienced for nearly a decade is exactly the same recruitment and abuse that is happening today. Maybe the approach is different with the internet, but the tactic, the manipulation, and the target are all the same.The weakest and most vulnerable are the ones who are preyed upon and we must be mindful of those people around us.

"It's one of the greatest gifts you can give yourself, to forgive. Forgive everybody." ~ Maya Angelou

Who am I?

Why on earth did this happen to me? These are
questions I asked myself for years, they are the same
questions you all still ask me today.

So who is Tanya Michelle?

Well, first off, I'm the young girl who was victimized
and didn't know any healthy ways to cope with people
at all. I was the loner at school, the outcast of my
family, and the one who felt unloved and unworthy
most of my life. Because of this, I was needy and
predators took advantage of that vulnerability in me. I
didn't meet some evil person lurking at the park, in the
bushes, I wasn't kidnapped from a dark street, or while

away on vacation. Although that does happen, more so then I would like to admit. I was lured by a stranger who was able to groom me for what was to come, by earning my trust. As you will read between the pages of this book, my childhood made me the perfect target for these predators! A girl named Rachel was the first, she groomed me- and Yes grooming is the perfect word to describe what had happened to me. It means she earned my trust, showered me with attention, and made me feel important and special. That misplaced trust and friendship is what lured me into the sex trade.

Why did Rachel's methods work?

I've really had to dig deep within myself to answer that question. For so long I haven't identified as being a child trafficking victim, you see, for many years I just saw myself as a prostitute. One that changed the way she earned a living. No more, no less. How very sad really. I now see very clearly, I was a victim! Rachel found me in my weakest moment. I felt hopeless and helpless child. I didn't feel like anyone understood or even cared about me. No family or friends. Ditched in some Treatment Center. This new friend asked questions, she listened to me and made so many promises. She talked about how we would be friends for the rest of our lives. With her I received the attention I was yearning for so badly for years!

Out of The Shadows is a story of a survivor of Human Trafficking in Canada. It is my story!

MAMA

My mother stares out of a picture with such an emptiness in her eyes. The picture is old, torn and starting to fade. I have taped it back together and placed it behind the plastic protection cover of my only childhood photo album. I had ripped the picture years ago in a moment of anger. The day I decided I was never going to speak to my mother again. I have had to take most of these pictures out of my parents home, on visits throughout the years in order to even have them in my possession. I rarely ever look at these now, choosing to leave them in the past.

In this photo, my mother is holding me, I appear to be only a few months old. I'm dressed in a dingy sleeper that had faded long before the picture was taken. I'm sitting on her lap, her hands are holding me, but not really supporting me, you know what I mean? My head, falling to the side uncomfortably. She seems to stare out beyond the camera and beyond whoever is trying to capture this moment. She doesn't seem interested really, in the least.

This photograph now tells me everything I need to know about my mother. Things as a young girl, I would never have noticed and certainly wouldn't have understood it. But I see it now as an adult, It's so crystal clear. She is expressionless and appears to be so very detached from me, that little baby girl that is sitting on her lap, and from whatever else was going on around her at that time.

I'm not even sure where this picture was taken, is she back home with her family in Newfoundland? Or still with my father in Ontario, still hiding the fact I even existed. It looks as if someone has placed me on her lap against her will. Her body language is screaming, " Take this baby away from me." Any other mother in a similar situation would be filled with love and excitement, eager to show off her firstborn child, Glowing really. But Not my mother, it appeared now and in fact almost every single picture that I have of us when I was young; She always looks so detached and empty. She is void of that motherly pride. Her gaze always seems to be anywhere but on me.

In the few pictures I have looked at of my brother and I as children, the pose is always the same, babies on her lap, Distance in her eyes. There is no real intimacy, she doesn't seem to cuddle up to us or beam with Pride for her children. I never really noticed that before.

Now most of us don't remember our early years, at least not entirely. We piece together a story about how we grew up through photos taken, pieces of memories and things that we are told. Some of my memories are so vivid though, like as if burned into my soul. What happens in those early years, of any child's life, is so vital. From birth to five years old, those years seemingly unimportant, set the stage for your life.

Those moments and events form the way we, as children, view the world around us and form ideas about attachment and about relationships with others. All I really remember from my childhood years is fear, violence, and pain.

I don't really ever remember seeing tenderness or intimacy between my mother and my father ever as a little girl, I really just really remember tension and anger, sometimes even hatred. They shouted at each other or didn't talk at all. There seemed to be a fight daily or my father was always in one of his moods. We as children always seemed to walk on eggshells, not wanting to anger anyone. In the end, I learned to block out all the fighting and all the abuse. In those really scary moments as a little girl, when I wanted my father to protect me, not hurt me, I would leave my body. I would leave my little body and watch from the ceiling- I truly believed all families lived like this.

In our own way, each of us was affected by the violence and the disciplinary parenting. My brother and I used to huddle together in one of our rooms and cry. We would continuously plan to run away and get out of that place.

One memory always stands out for me as that little girl. Years later in my life when a therapist asked about my first memory of my father, it was always the same one that came racing to the surface anytime anyone asked me about him; The image of a little five-year-old girl, maybe I'm not even five. Standing there in front of this man, that I don't think I even realize is my father, and I'm terrified! I had wet the bed that morning and was too afraid to tell my mother, like the previous mornings. Since our move to this strange place, with this strange man, I've begun to have accidents. My father had come into the bedroom that morning and discovered my mess. He became enraged and started to yell at me, this little girl, so scared of this stranger, who was my father. He forced me to drop my little panties and bend over my bed. That's the first time I remember leaving my body and floating to the ceiling. That was the first time I experienced the belt and the wrath of an angry father. These types of punishments continued for years. This was what they knew. This is how parenting was done. Children were seen and not heard.

This man was supposed to be a loving man sent to protect me and keep me safe and instead this man kept me scared and a shell of the person I was meant to become. My father, without even realizing it, I'm sure, set me up for predators and violence. He taught me that men were allowed to hurt me, control me and have me live in fear. He taught me that I was worthless and had no opinion of my own. And my mother, well she was probably fearful too and did nothing to stop what was happening. She to this day has never taken ownership and would rather place blame on others around her.

Now I don't say these things to hurt my parents, I mean God knows I have made my own mistakes as a parent and continue to make mistakes. I mean we are all human and . I believe my parents did the best they knew how with the skills and support they had at the time. Through a childhood of poverty and abuse, I formed beliefs that would write the script of my life. At thirteen I left home with children's services to escape the chaos and traded in a childhood of violence and fear for a decade-long run with Predators who took advantage of me and filled my life with more violence then I could ever have imagined. I never thought I would ever escape.

I did not dare to dream of brighter days ahead. I followed dangerous, illegal and destructive demands of a brutal and controlling pimp for many years. These demands ultimately cost me years of my childhood. The greatest price of all, however: I lost the ability to parent my first born daughter. Too damaged by my abuser to have any strength to fight. This is a consequence I pay for each day as I rebuild my life and the relationship with my her! And to protect our very fragile relationship, I want to keep her appearances throughout this book to a minimum.

While working through my painful past, I am able to see through all the lies and disbelief I had always held about myself. I see the actual truth now . The truth, I discovered, is that I am an intelligent, compassionate, loving and creative woman. I am capable of loving and caring for myself. I am a good mother, a faithful friend and a servant of God. I also realized that I can only go as far as I dare to dream. So I dream Big now, I have found hope again.

Who is this beautiful little girl? I see pictures of
myself, although I don't have many and I can't help but
wonder about her, who is she? She looks so sweet and
innocent, almost happy.
"How can these possibly be pictures of me? How did
life get so turned around now?"

Only small segments of my childhood come in and
out of my memory now- and the little I do remember
rarely makes me smile, if ever. One vivid, typical
memory: Little Tanya, crying and frightened. Wanting
to just hide away from her torment. My father is angry
about something, my little brother and I are about to
get the belt. He is standing over me, foaming at the
mouth he is so angry. His belt slips out of his belt loops
with such ease, I don't even really take notice until I feel
the sting on the backs of my legs, he missed my ass,

which is what I'm sure he was aiming for. I may be all but five or six years old. All I want is my mommy to come and rescue me, she never came ever.

Otherwise, the memories I have before the age of about ten years old have been recreated from pictures and other people accounts. I look at photos of my dad playing with us; I struggle to recall the sense of fun we had as a family. Clearly, we seemed to be having fun at this moment. I mean I'm sure my mom and dad loved me when I was a child but I can't bring an image to mind of This little girl inside me ever feeling loved.

I know I was born in North York, Ontario and raised up for the most part in a small village town in Northern B.C. My father was a coal miner back then. I am the oldest of three. My little brother is almost a year younger than me, to the day. His birthday is a day before mine. My baby sister was born much later, a decade actually. She was fortunate to not have to bare witness to a lot of these things that my brother and I both experienced. Her childhood memories are much different from ours.

Until I was around five years old we lived in Newfoundland, My mom, a single mother at the time. Her and my dad had split shortly after I was born and she was pregnant with my baby brother. I can't recall what my mom did for work if anything. She was always very vocal about us not having enough money and how we had to save everything. There never seemed to be enough. I remember being left alone as small children, not because my mother was unfit but maybe because she was working or sleeping from working. I say work, but I really don't know. Maybe looking back she was just depressed and stayed in bed a lot. I really don't know because I honestly don't know my mother at all.

When I was five, my mother and father reconciled and we moved to British Columbia with my father. A man that was essentially a stranger to my brother and I.

As a little girl, this man was a giant in size and scary as hell. All I can really remember from that time was Fear.

My dad made sure we never wasted anything growing up. I remember heat being a luxury unless coming from the wood stove, that was in the boot room attached to his trailer. With sternness in his voice, he told us, "We can't afford this heater to be turned on." He pointed to the thermostat on the wall. I remember the trailer always feeling cold. We had that wood stove but it really didn't do much for the other rooms in the house. I hated the cold so much. I longed for heat. One morning early before everyone was awake, I flicked that switch on the wall and heat blew out from under my feet from a vent on the floor. The heat warmed my ice cold toes. I could still hear my father's voice in my head but didn't understand why. Every morning before the house came alive I would flick that little switch on the wall and hover over that vent in the floor and get warm.

The day came when my dad got the bill in the mail. He walked in the house after work, I could tell he was already in a bad mood, Probably fighting with my mom. Barely even saying hello before he was standing in the kitchen, ripping open the mail. Suddenly he was standing in front of me screaming. "Who's been turning on the heat? I felt my heart nearly leap out of my chest, Panic rose in my belly. "Which one of you has been so selfish?! We don't have money for this." My eyes filled with tears; I didn't know that little switch on the wall cost money. I was so scared, to tell the truth, scared to let anyone know how selfish I was. The sadness became overwhelming and I cried out, "I'm sorry daddy, I'm sorry, please don't be mad, I didn't mean to do it." My father's face was filled with rage.

I can't remember exactly what he said after that, but his message was loud and clear, that's for sure: Tanya, this little girl, is not worth the money it takes to stay warm, she is very selfish and thinks only of herself. That little inner voice of mine repeated that message

over and over until it was ingrained into my whole self.
"I'm so worthless, I don't even deserve to be warm." I
am almost sure that at that very moment, I made the
decision to always put everyone else before me. If I care
for others more, than my father will be proud of me
and I won't be selfish anymore.

Nothing outside of our home made me feel any better
either. Kids in the neighborhood were cruel and teased
me constantly. Sometimes they were nice but that never
lasted long and only seemed to be when they wanted
something. I was constantly shunned by the other kids
and they convinced me they were all better than I was. I
pretended I had friends, I really didn't. I hated it here
and couldn't wait for the day to come when I could
escape. I daydreamed of it often and my cousin, Jenny
Lynn and I would swing on the swings at the park and
dream of our lives when we were all grown up, making
all of our own decisions. I can almost hear the birds and
smell the air in those memories. Swinging on swings,

singing at the top of our lungs and me, dreaming of a
life far away from here.

**

At 13 I had finally had enough and decided I wanted out. I ran away from home that fall day, with no intention of ever going back. I'm not sure who had let their parents know my plan but it wasn't long after school had let out that my dad had come looking and found me out on the back road heading for the next town. The next few hours are kind of a blur, I leave my body when in conflict with my dad. I do know that he has been talking with my mother as she sobs n the kitchen, I hear him say, "Just make the call Bet, If she doesn't want to be here we are not making her stay. If you don't want her out on the street then get someone here to pick her up." He tosses me a side glare from the kitchen. I'm seated, frozen with fear in the dining room. This is really the first time I have shown any rebellion towards my dad, I was refusing to stay!

I heard my mother dialing a number and speaking softly into the phone. A few hours later there was a strange woman at our door. My mother had packed a bag of my things and brought them down as the doorbell rang. My father stayed in the basement, not even wanting to look at me.

"This is Shelly Tanya, She is a social worker from Houston and she is here to pick you up." My mom said.

"Hi Tanya, I'm Shelley," She said "You are going to come with me and we can talk on the drive. Does that sound ok?" She asked as she grabbed my bag from the floor. My mom was crying a little as we headed for the car in the driveway.

"I have a bed for you at a group home in Houston Tanya". There are other girls your age there, you will make friends, we will get you back into school as soon as we can." Shelley smiled as we left my small northern town and headed down the highway. I never looked back.

Starting at a new school is always hard, but starting toward the end of the school year, a foster kid, new to town. When you're thirteen years old, well that is even harder. I mean everyone has already made their friends and new girls are quickly excluded from everything.

It was due to placements, paperwork and court dates that it took me a while to even get back into school; five months, to be exact. I just had been kicking back at whatever group home or foster home they dumped me in up until now.

Despite the delay getting back into school, it was all so rushed in the end. My social worker had enrolled me on a Friday and here I was in school on Monday. We rushed around over the weekend. Getting my supplies and new clothes. I didn't take much when I left home.

I was nervous as hell as I walked through the front doors of Houston Secondary on that Monday morning. I headed straight to the office, so nervous. I had never been to another school before. The teachers were not very welcoming, that's for sure. I had barely given them my name before they were telling me if my attendance was bad, I would be kicked out. I was shocked to have adults at school speak to me this way. They took me to some office to talk with someone about all the time I had missed and help me choose my classes. I have missed a ton of school and feel so far behind. Im grateful for the time and the help.

The first morning was spent in class with a girl named Cindy, She seemed nice but the class sucked, I hated it. Other students were acting so wild in the class, it literally made me so uncomfortable.

Within the first day a native girl had already targeted me for Bullying. Jackie was known at the school for picking on the new kids and she was on me as soon as i arrived. You would swear that girl knew i was coming. I just remember being so afraid of her. She was a couple grade ahead of me and loved to hip check me into lockers and torment me on my walks home from school. The thought actually makes me laugh out loud now.

I started drinking when I was thirteen. It numbed the pain of being in foster care. My parents making really no effort to fix anything and get me back home. I felt so unloved and unwanted. The mind numbing effect of alcohol was just what i needed to forget it all. I always found ways to get booze for the parties, study nights and movie hangouts. So there I was a young teenager, trying to fit in with a whole new crowd, in a whole new town. My confidence and self-worth took even a bigger shit kicking since arriving here and I was doing whatever I could to just fit in. My grades took a huge hit. The subjects I had excelled in before were barely holding on- Yet another failure to add to the list of many. The only thing I was learning to do now was, get smokes, booze and cash from whatever foster home or group home I was in.

The reward for my efforts? Acceptance from the other children at school. Looking back now all of this set me up for what was coming. The bullying, the drinking, the rape by the boy at school after being invited to study. So much of my life changed that day when Child Welfare showed up at my home! The feeling Worthlessness really started once I was raped! Everything seemed to get worse after that.

***

Hot water is starting to fill a bathtub. It's not my bathroom at home, I'm in someone else's bathroom. The water pouring into the tub and the steam rising is almost hypnotizing. I've left my body again, I am watching from the ceiling. I am looking down at this young, naked girl. She is crying, careful to not make a sound as she has been told. Her body is shaking as she steps into the tub and sits.

Fear of being discovered, shame for what had just happened and total anger of what she could not get back. Bright red blood can be seen in the water now. The young man walks in and I am unwillingly back in my body.

"I'm sorry Tanya, I didn't know. Like, you should have said something." All I could do was stare at him, with tears streaming down my face, "I did." I cried out. "Shhhh," He says. " My family is downstairs and I don't want them to know you're here. Hurry up and get dressed and I'll drive you home." Nathan says. He makes it sound as if he is doing me a favor.

I dry my soar, naked body numb and still a little dazed. I slip into my clothes that lays crumpled on the floor. "I have to get you outta here without my aunt seeing you." Nathan cautions. There was none here when I arrived a few hours earlier to study and watch a movie. Time had literally stopped for me. It stopped the moment he wouldn't hear, No. It stopped the moment he raped me. I was thirteen years old. I have been in the foster care system for less than six months. No one knew. I never told. This is the first time i have ever spoke of it. I was glad when my social worker sent me to my next placement a few towns a way. I never had to see him again.

***

The second time it happened, I refused to believe it for a very long time. How could i have let this happen again? And just a few short months since Studying with Nathan.

He had grabbed me from behind, around my neck. I never saw his face. I could only smell the rum and coke, wet across my cheeks, a scent that to this day still makes my insides clench and my throat close tight in fear.

I tried to fight. I was overpowered. Pulled into a dark, grassed space and violated, two blocks from my group home. I lay fixated on a church steeple in the distance, left wondering how this could be happening. I leave my body yet again.

He lifts his body from mine, he swears and kicks me. I had stopped moving when i left my body. Stopped screaming into the hand closed around my mouth so hard i would be staring at purple shadows of his fingertips on my cheeks for more than a week.

I lay there for what seemed like forever, before picking myself up, trying to repair my clothes and remember why the hell i had even been there.

Candy. I had been walking to the store to buy candy. Just a ten minute walk from the house. I berated myself all the way back to the house and then back into the night again because I had slipped on another girls shoes when I had darted to the store and suddenly became obsessed with finding the one I had left behind.

Maybe, I thought i could fix this one thing, put the shoes back where i found them, it would be as if the night never happened. I came across it discarded on the grass, marking where I had lost yet another part of my soul. I carried it home, still bleeding, then sat in the shower until the hot water ran cold and the cold water ran numb.

Again shame fills me and I said nothing. I report it to noone. I hadn't seen his face. I was not yet fourteen and was walking alone late at night. What did I think would happen?

A hesitant attempt to talk a girlfriend confirmed it. "Why were you walking so late?" I know now that question comes from a place of needing to feel safe: "What did you do wrong, so this doesn't happen to me too?"

But asked while I was still so raw it hurt to sit, that only planted a seed of rage. It wasn't at all my fault and yet my actions were under review. I shoved it as far back in my mind as I could, buried it under bad decisions and denial.

I had been suicidal for many months before I was raped. Maybe I wore the pain on my sleeve, maybe it made me an easy target. Maybe I cared so little about my life that I put myself into dangerous situations. I don't know. What I do know is that after nearly two weeks of trying to pretend I didn't care what had happened to me, the final straw was that I had a nice day. After enjoying my afternoon, the face I saw reflected in the mirror was so alien to me I couldn't imagine attaching myself to it anymore.

I tried to kill myself with a bottle of Tylenol, four Advil, and a 12-ounce can of Coke not long after the rapes. I wrote a four page suicide letter in Hot Pink "gel" ink — a note of explanations and apologies — folded it up, placed it in my right back pocket, and headed to the park, where I sat at a picnic bench and poured the red and yellow capsules into my hand.

I still remember the names on that note: Mom, Dad, Nan, Da, Jimmy and Chelsea. I remember wanting them to know I was sorry. I remember wanting them to know how desperate I was, how much pain I was in. I remember wanting them to know it was not their fault.

I took 4, 5, and 6 pills at a time.

Handful of pills; gulp of soda. Gulp of soda; handful of pills.

I had always hated taking pills, but suddenly it was easy. Handful after handful, down they went like candy. By the time I finished everything in front of me, my face was starting to tingle. My hands were shaking and wobbly, and I couldn't quite get my feet to do what I wanted them to.

I took so many pills I gagged as they went down my throat.

I took so many pills I thought I would surely get sick from the sugar in the soda before I was finished.

I took so many pills a phantom lump formed in my neck, in that spot where you feel the fluid push through after a hard swallow.

It wasn't a half-hearted attempt or a cry for help. I thought I would die. I wanted to die, but I didn't.

You see, my body fought for me when my mind no longer could. Even then God had a plan, His hand was on my life, even in that moment. My body forced the pills up, and while it took nearly two days of throwing up at hourly intervals, I came out of it alive. Five pounds lighter and a million times more depressed and confused, but alive.

But I didn't wake up because I was strong or smart or had some secret will to live.

I woke up purely by chance.

I woke up purely by luck.

I woke up because I got the formula "wrong."

I wasn't happy to be alive. In fact, when I opened my eyes and saw the nicotine-stained drop ceiling of my foster home hanging overhead and felt the bile race through my stomach and into my throat, I tried to swallow it. I wanted to lay there and swallow it — I wanted to drown in my own vomit — but apparently it is impossible to asphyxiate yourself if you are fully conscious.

I felt like a failure. Nothing more than a "suicidal failure."

"Fuck," I thought. "What good am I if I can't even kill myself correctly?"

But after 48 hours of violent heaving, after emptying myself of every food and fluid you can possibly imagine, I was exhausted. I was numb. After days of my continued illness, my foster parents took me to a doctor. The doctor must have known, because he told them to give me as much time as I needed to feel better, that he'd rarely seen a flu so severe, and that I wasn't to return to school until I was ready.

It was the compassion of that doctor, who saw through my miserable silence and understood the kind of pain I was in, who saved me. That somebody could be so compassionate to me helped pull me through in the months that followed.

I was so young and yet carried the weight of so much. I felt like a failure as a daughter. I felt like a failure as a sister, and a friend. Hell, they for months had been trying to find someone who even wanted me. In that moment i wanted so badly to just die. Not seeing that i in fact had a whole huge life in front of me.

And while today I see myself as a "Trauma Survivor," I am more than that. Today I am someone born from the ashes of my traumatic life. And while I still struggle with Anxiety and PTSD, today I see myself as lucky.

In the last 20 years, I've learned why I didn't die that night. I've also learned that I permanently damaged my heart. It's a kind of scar I carry that nobody can see. But it's there, and almost 30 years later it's still as raw.

Im sure my social worker knew something was going on in the weeks that followed that suicide attempt. She was boarding me on a plane for Vancouver not long after. I was to spend 30 days at treatment center there. I would have spent 30 days anywhere but where i was, hiding the secrets i was hiding.

"Another boring day," I said as I hung out in the
courtyard. I had no friends and didn't know any of the
kids here yet. I was placed temporarily in The Maples
Adolescent Treatment center in Burnaby BC- Far from
the small village town, I had grown up in Northern
British Columbia. I wondered how long they planned
on keeping me here. In less than one year in the care of
the province, I have been in twenty-one placements, I
have moved around way to often. A week here, a week
there. They just can't seem to find me anything long
term for older kids in the child welfare system. Due to
the remote locations in the north, moves meant new
towns, which made enrolling in school next to
impossible. So here I was in a treatment center in
Burnaby that was more like Jail. Glad to be away from
the memories of what has happened up north but still

hiding from the invisible pain and shame that no one can even see.

I spent as much time as possible in the courtyard, even though it was fenced with chain link and barbed wire, it was better than inside listening to the screaming teens and ignorant staff. I had already experienced physical, sexual and verbal abuse, although I wasn't aware that it was abnormal. I struggled so badly with self-worth and loving myself. I was struggling and no one even noticed.

One morning I was standing in the courtyard before a group, my eyes closed, the sun shining on my face, warming my cheeks and wishing the day had ended already. It was the same feeling I had the day before and the day before that! A feeling that I was all too familiar with. In fact, this was the same feeling every single day for what seemed like for as long as I could remember.

"Hey there", a young girl said. I opened my eyes and stared at the most beautiful blonde haired, smiling girl. She had the most piercing blue eyes. She was so thin and so pretty. She was everything I had wished to be. She was wearing the cutest pink sundress and it was the perfect fit for her body.

"Hi", I said, surprised that she was even talking to me.

"I see you out here every morning all by yourself," she said, "And well you seem very sad and alone. I thought I would keep you company today." I mumbled something and she smiled at me.

"Is it ok if we talk?" I nodded, too excited to even know what to say to her or how to respond. She wants to talk to me. Maybe she wants to be my friend.

"You must be lonely here." before I had the chance to answer, she said. My name is Rachel and I'm seventeen, well almost eighteen." She held out her hand.

"What's your name?"

"Tanya." I shook her hand and inhaled the sweet scent of the hand cream she wore.

"Tanya is a nice name, How old are you?"
"Thirteen, well almost fourteen."

"Where's your family?" her voice was so gentle and warm as she continued to smile at me. Rachel leaned in closer as she spoke to me, I couldn't help but sense her really wanting to get to know me.

"My mom, dad, and siblings live up north," I said. " I have been in the care of the province for almost a year now." I shrugged.

I stood there in front of her, engulfed in my own thoughts, wallowing in self-pity, loneliness, and discontentment. (My usual way of thinking those days).

Immediately I liked her, she was so beautiful and confident. She was everything I was not and she was all I wanted to become. I was still in shock that she actually liked me and considered me her friend at all. I didn't see any of her flaws if she even had any and I didn't know if she could understand or even imagine the childhood I had experienced or the time in foster care leading up to this moment or why I was even here.

After that first encounter, I yearned to be exactly like her. Rachel had these intense blue eyes that made me feel as though she could see right through to my soul. I began to feel she was the older sister I never had and always wanted.

Rachel smiled at me once more, as if to say, "I understand and I'm sorry." Within those first moments of meeting. Rachel gave me hope and offered me friendship and support. No one had ever treated me that way, ever. I was bullied both inside and outside of my home; I had never had anyone stand up for me.

Looking back, I now know she chose me, even before she spoke one word to me. I'm, sure she spotted me the day I was brought in. She saw the longing in my eyes and the loneliness that I projected out of my hurts, trauma, and agony. As I learned later, Predators watch their victim before they target them. She was seeking me, the girl who was lonely and abused and showing my vulnerability in the way I walked, and the helplessness in my eyes. You see predators like Rachel, sense that lack of family connection or support. Only later could I see that my own identity was so fragile and distorted. Then I would realize that Rachel had chosen me because she knew I was vulnerable and lonely.

Rachel sat with me in that courtyard and we talked and talked for what seemed like hours. It really didn't take long at all for that girl to win my trust. She asked me all the right questions and focused on my eyes as I answered them. No one in my entire life had listened to me like that before, so intently.

She told me almost nothing about herself, which I didn't even really realize then. Her questions expressed such interest in me, something no one in my life had ever done. No one ever paid much attention to me. I was short, slightly overweight and I constantly sought approval from adults and older kids. That approval rarely came. Even if it did, the longing in my heart and soul was so desperate, the acceptance was never enough anyway.

As I stared at Rachel, I kept wishing I looked like her. She seemed so independent and strong, the type who could stand up for herself. Nothing at all like me. I could tell she too had a rough childhood from the references she had made to her parents and those authority figures in her life. And just like any other naive teenage girl, opened up quickly and spoke way to freely, happy to have someone older who would listen to me and care about my thoughts and feelings! Rachel related to my stories of abuse with comments like "Your dad really hurt you huh?" I know what you mean, my dad acts the same way. My dad did that too, he drinks way too much.

When I was around Rachel, I felt so completely grown up. She let me borrow her clothes and things and that made me feel even more like her, my role model, my idol, my sister. The past year had been so lonely. Moving was hard but having parents that didn't want to work on making things better and having you return home, was even harder. So this friendship was really an answer to my prayers. Someone who showed me some affection and treated me like family. I was thirteen, I mean what did I know.

Soon after our friendship began, I got a day pass and Rachel insisted she shows me the bright lights and the Big City. Remember I am from that small, northern town, I haven't really seen a city yet. I had never seen anything like what she was showing me. So large and so busy. Everyone seemed to be in a rush to get somewhere. We were heading to Stanley Park, she said.

To meet up with some of her friends that would now be my friends too!

When we arrived I could see a large group of people just past the park and down by the water. She pointed to a man in the group, the one that seemed to be the oldest, the leader. He was one of the most intimidating men I had ever seen. "I work for him." She said although she didn't say what she did for work. I was so focused on this man, who seemed to be in charge and fathering this large group of people. I didn't even think to ask her what her job was. This man was tall, with long dark hair pulled back into a ponytail and a shit ton of tattoos. He was by the water tossing rocks and laughing with some of the others. I couldn't help but wish I had a man like that, someone who thought laughing and spending time at the beach with me and the people he loved was important.

When Rachel finally introduced us, he smiled, held out his hand and said, " Hey there darlin, My name is

Pony." He introduced me to another girl they called Angel and his three-year-old son. Even though my dad was scary as hell and sometimes abusive, I knew in the back of my mind that not every dad was like that. I mean here was Pony, playing with his son, so in my young mind, he was a good man. He turned away from us and went back to playing with his son. I admired the casual way he related to him.

He was the kind of daddy I had wished I had.

That afternoon I was starving. Rachel had rushed me out on my day pass this morning and I missed breakfast. While Pony played with his son, I asked Rachel if I could have a dollar for the nearby vending machine. At the beginning of our friendship, Rachel had encouraged me to always ask for money when I was hungry.

Instead of handing me the change like she had done so many times before, she said, just loud enough for

Pony to hear, "He will give you anything you want." She nudged me towards him. "All you have to do is ask him girl."

"Could I have some change for the vending machine?" I asked Pony with hesitation. Even though he was a stranger to me, he seemed nice enough. And well, my best friend told me I could trust him. So I did.

"Of course." He reached into his pocket and pulled out a dollar bill. " Here," He said. I reached for the bill, but he held onto it for a few extra moments and smiled at me. Before he let it go, he said, "But one day you will owe me, darlin."

"What does that mean?"

"Don't worry Darlin, You will know when the time comes," He called out and smiled at me again. Even though he appeared to be teasing me, the words didn't sound right at all. "And I Don't want you to say no." As

Rachel and I walked to the vending machine, I asked, "What did he mean by that?"

"Oh girl, stop worrying, he's just playing with you." Rachel laughed, but this time her laugh seemed different, maybe she was nervous? I wasn't too sure. I mean he seemed very serious to me when he said it. I was confused. Maybe that's why those words, were ones I have never forgotten- You will owe me one day.

As I ate the stale potato chips from the vending machine, I didn't ask Rachel again about what Pony had meant by what he had said. But I'll tell you, something just didn't feel right. However, I quickly reminded myself that I never have to do anything I don't want to do. My little premature, childish, thirteen-year-old mind couldn't begin to imagine what he would want me to do anyway. I mean, It was only a dollar. How would he want me to pay that back? I chuckled at the thought. Even though at that moment I

didn't understand what those words meant. The day
would come when I would.

Rachel was grooming me, obviously, but I didn't have any clue what was really happening. The whole process took about a month. The same amount of time I spent in that treatment center. By then I had no doubt whatsoever that Rachel loved me like a sister and would do anything for me and for our new found friendship. Most mornings we met out in the courtyard. She always sat super close to me and we talked about my family and what I wanted to do and be when I grew up.

One day she finally asked, "Do you want to go back up north?". I haven't really given it a lot of thought! She said that we could live together in a small apartment downtown, All I had to do was say yes! I mean how would I say no, I loved my best friend and wanted to have a life outside of the system and group homes and bullshit.

After I Spent about a week with Rachel in her little apartment off of Granville street. Pony seemed to be there every night collecting money and cutting up dope. I had learned that Pony was not just running girls, he was running most of the drugs in downtown Vancouver. At thirteen, I didn't see the potential danger of the situation I was getting myself into.

He stopped by on this morning with breakfast and new shoes for Rachel, She had been eyeing them up a few days before, at the mall. Pony sat down beside me and said: "You'll be going out tonight with Rachel." He glanced at Rachel and winked. " You'll go down Robson Street. Teach our new angel the game!" Pony told her. He smiled at me and said, "Girl, you go with Rach, she's gonna show you what's up. She is my number one girl, she knows how to make money, so pay close attention."

Then he laughed and pulled Rachel to his lap. Rachel smiled as Pony whispered something to her quickly and hummed a song in her ear.

Rachel barely spoke to me as we drove to the corner of Robson and Seymour. As we got out of the car, Pony grabbed a few bills from the console and handed us each twenty bucks.

"Now Tanya, remember what I have told you, and listen to this bitch," He warned me. "You need to bring home Five Hundred a night. That's your trap, no less."

He had already spoken to me about my trap (How much money I had to make) earlier that morning and made it very clear what happens when we don't obey what he demands. Although this man terrified me most of the time, I couldn't help but have a deep, deep desire to please him. I wanted Pony to like me, I wanted him to be proud, I wanted to do well. Pony really was the man to make me feel pretty and smart and I loved when he gave me all of his attention. It was in those moments that I truly believed he loved me and wanted to protect me.

As we walked toward what appeared to be Ponys corner, Rachel asked us to make a quick stop. " There's a donair shop just down here," Rachel said as her pace grew faster. When we arrived, the place appeared to be closed. I was a bit confused but Rachel seemed calm. "Don't worry Tan," she said as she knocked lightly on the back entrance. "I wanted your first to be someone I knew would be nice to you." I didn't understand.

With that, a very large man, with a huge belly and predatory smile opened the door. I was immediately uncomfortable. I was praying that she didn't plan to have us here long. Rachel said, "Tan, give me just a minute, I'll be right back." She took the man's arm and they headed to the coffee area inside the restaurant. I followed her inside and sat at the nearest table. At first, I had thought we were heading to a date for her but it was soon clear that was not what was happening. I saw the man hand, Rachel, a wad of cash.

When they walked back to the table I was sitting at, the fat man just smiled at me and took my hand. He leads me through the donair shop to a back office with an old, dirty futon. It had an old pink blanket thrown over it to try and hide the stains. Rachel remained at the table, staring out the window, waiting for us to be finished.

The man sat down on the futon and motioned for me to join him. I was trembling. I forced myself to move toward him and the futon. I sure he sensed how I was feeling because he tried to smile at me and said, "Girl, don't be scared, this doesn't hurt, how old are you, sweetheart?"

Pony had always told me when Johns asked my age, I was to tell them the truth. He said they would pay more for my young juice. I didn't get it then.

"I'm thirteen." I crossed my arms over my chest and his eyes widened with excitement and I could see almost immediately his crotch in his chef pants start to bulge. This man liked that I was thirteen, it actually excited him. This man wanted me. I sat on the futon next to him and he started trying to kiss me and push his large, hairy hands down my pants to touch me. In the midst of his groping, he murmured " Suck my dick, little girl." After a moment's hesitation, his hand was on the back of my head. Pushing me down. He moaned, grabbed me, "Suck it hard", He said.

That floating feeling came over me again, The same floating feeling that had come over me many times before when dealing with the physical abuse of my father or the Rapes in my last two placements. I felt in those very moments that the real me was up above my body, watching what was happening as if to someone else other than me. I wasn't part of the hurt that was happening. I was just a spectator watching a thirteen-year-old child stroking a man harder and harder as he moaned in pleasure.

After he seemed to be finished and the groaning had stopped. I looked up at the door to see Rachel standing there watching us. The man quickly straightened his chef's jacket as she walked through the door. Grabbing my arm, she looked at me, "Come on Kid, it's time to go." She said.

The second customer of the night lived at a Motel nearby. He was rather tall and a little awkward. I listened intently as Rachel negotiated with him. "You looking for company tonight sweetheart? What are you looking for darling? She said, smiling up at him. She was so nice to him, like overly nice. I don't think I had ever seen Rachel treat a man like that before.

"I just want sex." He told her nervously.

"Well Hunny, It's your lucky night darling," Rachel said, glancing back in my direction. "She's coming with me, I'm showing her the ropes. Its one hundred for me and if you want her, well you better grab another hundred." He glanced over at me, shook his head, "Just you."

Rachel shot me a cocky smile.

I was glad he didn't want me, I wasn't over the fat guy, only an hour earlier. I mean I sure didn't want to have sex with him. But the biggest problem with that was that I wasn't getting any closer to the five bills Pony wanted at the end of the night. I knew based on the money Rachel was charging, I needed to go out with at least five men a night to make my money. Unless it was a lucky night and I had men that wanted to spend more. That would certainly make this night easier, so I told myself, I better get as much as I could from each one of these perverts.

After Rachel was finished with her first trick, we returned to Robson street and it was time for me to start my real work on the stroll. Standing with my shoes to the curb, smiling shyly as the men drove by. It was a long night. Most of the men who took us out that night had lots of money and were staying in hotels close to stroll, like the four seasons. They would walk down the street and we would chat with them as they walked by. I stayed close to Rachel so that I wouldn't lose her.

"This is Tanya, She's my new wifey. Pony has me showing her the ropes." Rachel smiled proudly as she introduced me to the other girls on the stroll. Pony was around but he was far from stupid; He didn't talk to any of us out on the stroll, but he did check on us. He drove my on several occasions but acted as if I was a stranger. Every couple hours I was to walk to the payphone up the street and call him, as he had instructed me to do when he drove us here tonight.

Rachel really only stuck close for a couple of days. After that, I was on my own, talking to men by myself and going with them to their hotel or for drives in their cars. There was also a boarding house a block away, that rented rooms by the hour and sometimes if tricks didn't have a place, I took them there.

Days turned into weeks and life took on a schedule and routine. I knew where I was going each day and what was expected of me. I needed to make money to keep Pony off my back, but for the most part, I felt like I belonged. I belonged to my man, I belonged to our family of girls and to this life. I no longer had to worry about where I fit in or where I would stay or how I would eat. All those things I felt like I had been looking for all this time, I had found right here on the streets of Vancouver, B.C.

The only downside to all of this was all the men. At first, I don't know how to handle it: I could feel my mind, heart, and soul going numb. Eventually, while my body was being used by these sick men, I would just continue to float to the top of the room, completely leave my body, separated myself from the horror that was my life. Just so I would survive.

Having friends and being popular- typical teenage problems, they quickly became twisted by the dark criminal world that I was now living each day. I was still just a child on the inside, a young little girl, who liked the same things all little girls liked. I loved pretty clothes and getting my nails done.

One night I sat warming up and eating some dinner before heading back out on the stroll. Another young girl rushed into the restaurant and sat down in the booth beside me. "Who did your makeup?" She asked as she fumbled with the sugar packets on the table. "I Love the way you did your eyes, that brown is seriously such a great color." In the next breath, she said, "Hey did you hear about Kevin?"

I frowned, I knew her man was named Kevin. One of the many rules I had learned was not to discuss your man down on the stroll. Pony was very clear that was a huge mistake and I was not to talk his business to anyone, ever.

"Cassie killed him." Cassie was another girl about Rachel's age I'm guessing. I blinked and was a little shocked. I mean Just like that, this girls man was dead-killed? Wasn't that murder? Where was Cassy? I didn't know what to say to her.

She stacked the little creamer containers on the table and continued with her story. "Cassie was so pissed at him, but I really don't think she meant to do it. She says she didn't mean to shoot him. She's been acting all kinds of crazy and hasn't even changed her clothes since it happened and the pigs came and took Kevin's body away. I'm just so glad they didn't take Cassy to jail.

She didn't really look up as she told her story. She just swung her feet under the bench seat and played with the cream and sugar on the table. Then we started talking about makeup again. It was hard not to feel so much confusion but that how it was with the game. Young Girls in really sexy clothes, doing very adult things while deep down they are still just children wanting to play dress up and wear moms makeup and high heels.

I never heard what had ever happened to Cassy after the death of Kevin.

I am standing beside Highway 16 outside Hazelton
BC. The hot sun shone bright. I was penniless,
frightened and 1,200 kilometers from Vancouver. It's
the wee hours of the morning, the sun is rising and I
am sticking my thumb out for a ride. I had been picked
up by the police a few days before and the crisis center
in Vancouver had stuck me on a plane, to a town I
hated, a social worker who could care less and a family
that clearly didn't want me and didn't want to repair
any of our relationship or family. I have no intention of
staying and am grateful that no one even bothered to
show up at the airport. Just another indication for a
young girl that she is unwanted.

It is 1990, I am 14 years old, and I am in a jam. I must
get to Vancouver. My mind is racing, I haven't spoken

to Rachel or Pony. They are probably thinking I'm in jail. It is a Sunday, in the days before ATMs and Email Money Transfers or even cell phones for that matter. I haven't got a cent on me.

These days they call the Highway 16, The Highway of Tears. Over the last 30 years, some 40 women, have gone missing from it, never to been seen again. I didn't know it back then, but five women had disappeared already from this exact stretch of highway. I don't think I could have stood there knowing that. Now, thinking back on that day, I cringe with what might have been. The thought sends shivers down my spine. God has clearly had a hand on my life.

My first ride came in minutes: A high school teacher heading to Hazelton, three hours east. We paralleled the wide, grey-blue, fast-moving Skeena River. He was the father of a teenage daughter, the same age as me. "You shouldn't be doing this," he said. "It is not safe." But somehow I was lulled into a feeling of security by the ease and comfort of this first ride. All would be fine.

He dropped me off beside a weigh-scale station, saying,

"Call your parents, Please."

I stood outside Hazelton. And stood and stood. The

longer I stood, the more paranoid I became. It would be

so easy to disappear from this ribbon of highway that

links small towns and villages, Hop in a car and is gone

forever. At least the weigh scale station master was

watching me. He could describe any car or truck that

picked me up to the police, I rationalized with myself.

More than an hour passed. My paranoia grew. I hid

my knife under my shirt so no one could see it. Twenty

minutes later a black Jimmy GMC with Playboy Bunny

mud flaps pulled beyond me and honked. I picked up

my backpack and ran. He was in his early 30s, flashing

gold jewelry, and smelling of aftershave and breath

mints. "I'm going to Burns Lake," he smiled. I threw

my backpack in the truck bed and hopped in.

After about an hour, he pulled into a roadside park. "I have something that will help with your nerves." He hopped out of his side. I hadn't paid much attention to him until then, but as he jumped out of the truck I suddenly saw that despite a normal-sized torso, he was only about four feet tall. He was driving with hand controls as his legs couldn't reach the gas and brake pedals. He came back, swinging himself up unto the seat with his muscular arms, and showed me a white powder wrapped in cellophane. "Try this," he said as he pulled out the rearview mirror, took out a razor and cut up lines of cocaine.

It is only now that I shake my head in disbelief: I was riding with a coke-snorting midget!

Back then, I shook my head, declining. I'd never done drugs and I wasn't going to start now. I was in enough trouble already.

"Suit yourself," he grumbled. He stopped about every 40 minutes to do another line and when he finally dropped me off at a gas station outside Burns Lake he seemed glad to be rid of me.

My next ride came in minutes, another concerned father, a vacuum cleaner salesman. He paid for and watched me eat an omelet in a German-themed diner and pressed $20 into my hand before he left me by the side of the road near a shimmering stand of aspen, I am not exactly sure where.

It was around 7 pm and I still had some 200 miles to go. A beat-up orange Toyota Tercel pulled over. Behind the wheel was a blond, tousle-haired man, maybe age 25 or so. He looked like a scruffy, dissolute, slightly older version of my university pals.

I hopped in. It was only then I noticed the opened case of beer behind the seat, half of the 24 bottles already consumed. "I'm going to Vancouver," he slurred.

He chatted about his summer job as a logger, his loneliness working in the bush, how he'd always go to PG on his days off. I was so exhausted I finally fell asleep, one hand resting on my hidden Buck knife under my shirt.

I woke up when I suddenly felt the bumpiness of a gravel road instead of smooth blacktop. He had left the highway. We were going off on some desolate side road.

Fear surged inside me. I was instantly awake. I pulled my knife from its sheath, turning on him.

"What the FUCK do you think you are doing!!" I yelled, brandishing the blade at him.

His stricken eyes said he feared exactly what I had feared all day: I'm going to be knifed by some jumped up weirdo!

"I just have to pee," he whimpered.

I looked around. We were about 15 meters off the highway on a gravel road.

"Oh, okay," I said, sheepishly. "You can pee"

I put my knife away. We laughed nervously. He went out and did his business and we were back on the road.

Dusk was falling and the rocky, scrubby landscape was getting familiar. An hour later he dropped me off at the Sky Train Station in Surrey. "Can I call you sometime? he asked. And then I knew just how lonely one could get in the bush, up north, if you would ask out a girl who had pulled a knife on you.

"Sorry, I don't have a phone. I am living in Vancouver with friends." I said. "But thank you so much for the ride, really, I appreciate it and sorry if I scared you back there." Referring to the Pee break.

Just four years later, I'm in Edmonton and see a Picture flash across the news screen of a girl in my community who had died on that same stretch of highway. It is then that I learn for the first time about the history of that highway and the nickname, Highway of Tears. Another brush with death. Something I have encountered more times then I want to admit.

Every time I scroll Face book and see a post or I come across the documentary that is on netflixs, I am reminded just how grateful I am to be alive and blessed to to have become just another statistic. Another sign of God's hand on my life.

The weeks turned into months and before you knew
it, it had been a couple years and I continued to work
on the streets of Vancouver. Now I was sixteen so that
Hypnotic bullshit that worked when I was a child and
seems to keep tied to Pony had weakened. I only
continued to work for him out of fear. Even then, there
were times I vowed I wouldn't return and that I was
leaving. But it was almost as if I was drawn to him, like
a moth to a flame. I couldn't seem to control myself.

A small part of me knew he was evil and would only
cause me extreme pain. At the same time, I couldn't
help but feel as if he was the only person on the face of
the planet to accept me and all of my flaws. He was the
only man that truly loved me. Regular people seemed
to know, and they looked at me disgusted; I had seen it
with my own eyes every time the night turned into day

and I was still on the stroll. When women would be rushing by to get to work. I could see their mouths turn down as they approached me and hear their whispers: "Look at that! Wow, what is she wearing? Like the nighttime has ended, Whore!"

Pony was right, regular people hated me and would never accept me. Just like he always said, "Once a Ho, Always a Ho."

I certainly was nothing like the regular teenager. Literally growing up on the streets of Vancouver, for the most part. I had turned into an adult even though there was a part of me that remained a child, almost like being frozen in time, unable to make my own choices or do anything for myself. I learned everything from Pony. But because he always seemed to keep moving me to different hotels or apartments around the city, I never really learned how to do the basic things. Nothing was ever celebrated. Not birthdays or any other holidays, for that matter. Not even Christmas. I truly had no idea what was happening in the world outside of "The Game" and I was learning from life on the streets.

I couldn't imagine sitting in a classroom again. I missed my friends, I missed my favorite teacher, Mr. Sutter. But what I found I missed most was the library, filled with books. You see as a young child before Pony and Rachel, I loved to read. I loved to devour books and transport myself to another time, another place, just by flipping through the pages. I would pick up paperbacks now from the local smoke shop on the stroll or I would find them in dates homes and they would find there way into my purse. I shared these books with other girls on the stroll too. Some hadn't read a book in years.

Sometimes Pony would catch me reading. I wouldn't even notice him because I would be so deep into the story and my thoughts. I wouldn't notice until he ripped the book from my hands.

"I've told you, Bitch! You don't need to fucking read! You just love getting into trouble, don't ya darlin? He would stand over me screaming, hands balled into fists, staring down at me. I could almost feel the anger radiating from his body.

"You're a dumb bitch, you know that? You're a Whore! What do you think reading is going to do? Answer me!"

I stayed completely silent, head down, confused if I should give him an answer or not. He would push and slap me. "What are you going to say, bitch? That's right not a damn thing. You're just a whore and only good for one thing."

Books were my salvation. They provided relief from a life I did not want to be living, they were a respite from worrying about the secrets I carried with me. I used books the way I would use other, more harmful escapes later in life. They were a way out of the pain of the story I was living, a story written largely by the unreliable narrators in my life. They offered up an alternate universe in which I didn't have to hide who I was and what had happened.

I never thought I would tell my shame stories, let alone share them in the chapters of a book. Those secrets held me back and kept me small. The weight of them was crushing. I spent most of my lifeguarding them and making sure no one really saw me.

The thing is, those stories demand to be told. The truth is nothing if not insistent. My secrets were making themselves known in toxic and harmful ways in my life – addiction, fear, Abuse, Human trafficking, control, rape, unhealthy relationships... All of those things were my story being told – I just wasn't the one telling it.

When I finally became unable, and eventually, unwilling, to keep those secrets anymore, I became a storyteller. By sharing my stories, by writing them down, by allowing myself to be seen in all my brokenness, I finally found healing and connection and joy.

What if the power to heal yourself has been yours all along? What if the secrets you've been carrying, those dark and heavy shame stories, are open to challenge? What would happen if you came to believe your stories are not unspeakable and you could survive the telling? What if you decided to tell the truth about your life story in order to write a new ending?

You can, you know.

We either own our stories, or they own us.

Period.

Something slammed shut above me, clicking into place. The noise brought me back to consciousness, waking me into an instant panic. My eyes flew open and my breathing labored and rugged. I was lying on my side, and it was dark. Too dark to see anything. My heart hammered with fear and I felt as if I was going to puke. Beads of sweat rolling down my face. The hard surface I was laying on hurting my hip. Where the hell was I? What was going on? Rough carpet rubbed against my cheek, irritating my skin. I reached up above me. I hit something hard. I pressed my palm against it. The air was hot and stale. No, this was not happening, it couldn't be. I was in the trunk of a car. I flipped over onto my back and began banging on the roof of the trunk.

"Help!" I pushed hard against the roof. I balled my hands into fists and pounded. Frantic, I banged on the roof of that trunk until my hands hurt. " Please help me!" There had to be a way out. I rolled over to my side and began frantically searching for the trunk release. I reached out in front of me, feeling the metal latch. "Please!" I cried, "Somebody help." I was going to die, I knew it. I would swelter and die in this trunk. I kicked my legs against the side of the trunk and screamed. Oh God, I would suffocate. The air was going to run out and I was going to suffocate and die. It would be a slow, horrible death. I swallowed a sob and kept my mouth shut. I needed to save the oxygen I had left.

As soon as I was still, I could hear muffled noises coming from the outside of the trunk. My muscles ached as I struggled to keep calm, while everything in me wanted to scream for help. Whoever was outside of that trunk would have heard me already and they didn't help me. They had to have been the two guys who put me here, I am having flashes now of being grabbed from the stroll. I moved my trembling hands over my face, pressed against my lips as my teeth start to chatter. Hot tears are silently streaming down my face. I move to the end of the trunk, trying desperately to hear what they are saying to each other and figure out what they want with me.

"I found her downtown." He said I didn't recognize his voice at all. " Pony was nowhere to be found, little bitch. Mark wants his money, I figured she was the next best thing." He said. " I thought at least with this bitch, you can make a statement. Pony has to pay his dope debt, period!"

"Help me!" I screamed as loud as I could. " Help, get me out of here! Help!!" Someone hits the car. "Shut the fuck up, you stupid whore!" He yelled, " No one can hear you." He taunted. Panting, I become very still. Nausea twisted in the pit of my stomach. "How far was I from stroll? Where the hell were we? It had to be secluded if no one could hear me. Then again, he could be lying. Taking in another breath of hot air, I screamed! I extended my arms desperately and clawed at the top of the trunk. The car begins to rock. "I said, shut the fuck up!" He screamed. " Peter!" A voice yelled. "Stop it." Peter must have taken his hands off the car, it had stopped shaking. I could hear shoes scuffling on gravel. I took in another shallow breath and listened.

"God dammit!" Peter started. " I swear to God I'm going-" he was cut off when the car phone rang. Clearly, we are in an expensive ride. Whos car is this? I swallowed hard and realized I was shaking uncontrollably. I pulled my arms to my chest. How the hell was I gonna get myself out of here? I was locked in a trunk, God knows where. Peter and this other man clearly had no intention of letting me out. I was going to die!

"Yes sir, we ran into a complication." I could hear him on the car phone. " We are taking care of it." My thoughts switched to Rachel. What was going through her mind? Had she started looking for me? What was going through her mind? I assumed it had been hours since anyone had seen me on the stroll, I have lost track of time. Fear bubbles up in my stomach. It wouldn't take long before they would notice I was missing. The police would be looking for me soon. Everything was going to be ok, I had to believe that.

Suddenly the trunk opens. I am, for a moment, blinded by the light in the trunk. I take in a huge breath of fresh air, adrenaline surges through my body. I push myself up, prepared to make a mad run for it but someone grabs my arms. "Going somewhere?" Peter sneered, His fingers digging into my skin. He smiles and twists my flesh in his hands.

"Get the fuck off me!" I scream and struggle to try and free myself. I turn my body and twist my arm, breaking free from his grasp. I curl my fingers into a fist and hit him as hard as I can. My blow is strong, but not nearly strong enough. The pain he felt only fueled his rage. IN a swift moment, he brought his hand back and slapped me hard across the face. Still, I didn't give up. I wrapped my fingers around his wrist and pressed my nails into his skin before dragging them down his arm. Peter grunts in pain and headbutt me. My ears ring and I am disoriented. I open my mouth to scream as his hands wrap around my throat. My voice dead, my throat burning as his grip tightens. My pulse pounded against his hands. I brought my hands up in a desperate attempt to break free from his grasp.

My vision blurs, I lose the strength in my hands. My arms flop to the side. My body shutters and I strain for a breath. My eyes quickly dart to the other man. He is standing a few yards back. His arms are tightly crossed across his chest. His dark eyes conveying nothing but pure rage. I hated him for just standing there doing nothing. Just when I thought I was about to pass out, Peter released his hands. He kept his eyes, however, locked on mine. My legs felt heavy and my movements slow from the lack of oxygen. He tipped his head and ran his fingers down my arm. His touch, now, deliberately gentle. He fingers the hem of my tank top for a few seconds before slipping his hand under. His eyes closed as he drags his hand up over my stomach.

Hot tears fall from the corner of my eyes. His skin against mine makes me sick. My vision is still clouded. His fingers reach my bra and he hesitates, I'm sure enjoying the build-up he is creating in his mind. He pushes his hand up and groans when his fingers are wrapped around my breast. Unable to scream, I let out a low whimper. Peter licks his lips and pinches my nipple. These men always seem to have this need to torture me. I leave my body.

I'm not sure how much time has passed when the second car rolls up. A man steps out and yells, "Peter, Robin, What the hell, are you guys fucking stupid?" He approaches the trunk.

"Please!" My voice breaks. " I just want to go home. Please!" This man quickly helps me out of the trunk. " Girl, you need to go find your man," Mark instructed. " He owes me five grand and I want it, You hear me?" He was writing his phone number on a piece of a cigarette pack. " You find him and you have him call me. They will be back if he doesn't." He drops me in the alley on the stroll. I collapse against a dumpster, overcome with such fear and sadness. I just want to die.

I head to find Pony fast.

I noticed a light-skinned man, with corn rows in his hair. He had the most intense stare. He was just standing there watching the girls go back and forth working the stroll. I recognize him, I think. None of the other girls even raised a glance to him as they knew he was "live". He had on this bright green and black tracksuit with crisp white Nike kicks. He seemed to be waiting for us because when he saw Rachel and I approaching, he smiled and called out to Rachel. Oh my God, it was one of those men that had been there when I was kidnaped a week ago. He was the one who didn't help me or stop his friend Peter. He was the one that had come and met with Pony after Mark had dropped me off to go find him. I was so confused

Rachel and this Robin exchanged a few words. I saw money exchange hands. Rachel approached me. " This here is Robin, You're going with him now." This was the moment I was sold to a PIMP, I'm Sixteen years old and should be getting ready to start my last year of high school.

"Robin?," I raised my eyebrow. The man's stare had me in a trance or something. It was like for the first time someone could see me, not this broken shell of a person, but me!

"Hey there beautiful," He said, "How would you like to head to the Island with me? It's really nice there. I'll take you there with me and show you the city, ok? I'm gonna show you the Real Game Sweetheart."

We headed to the Island that very night on the last ferry leaving Tsawwassen. The ferry ride is just over an hour and a half. We were not alone, Robin was traveling with his bro. The driver, his name was Mark, drove us in his Big, Gold, Cadillac. I sat in the backseat with my eyes to the floor. I had never seen men like this or a car like this for that matter. I could tell it was expensive. These men made Pony seem small. These were serious mother fuckers, I could tell.

From the way Mark was driving and handling this huge caddy, I could sense his pride in his car.

"When am I going to see Pony and Rachel again?" I asked as I reached to roll down my window. I couldn't believe how many buttons were on the door. Robin firmly pushed my hand away. "Stop touching things, girl."

"Sorry." I was so stupid, I had already made him mad. He shook his head and went back to talking with Mark. I was just so relieved he wasn't yelling at me. After a few more minutes he answered my question. "You're not going to see them anymore. That Bitch and his Ho are off to Toronto, They are Addicts, You are with me now."

As we lined up to drive onto the ferry that would take us to Victoria I began to relax. Robin was good looking, in this like flashy gangster kinda way. His voice was as smooth as silk when he spoke to me. There was just something that made me trust him. He asked me a ton of questions and really seemed interested in what I had to say.

"How did you end up with those clowns? I mean girl, you are a stallion. You weren't making nearly the bank you should have. I looked out the window as the ferry docked. I had never made anything. Pony always took my money, so it really didn't make a difference. Money was really not that important to me. I was just excited about a ferry ride and another city.

After a few more minutes, Robin asked, "Where are your parents? Did you run away from home or something?" I felt my heart fall to the pit of my stomach. "No, no, nothing like that. I just had to get outta there and really they don't care, they never even bothered to come to look, it's been years!" I shifted uncomfortably in my seat and looked out the window as Mark pulled us onto the ferry.

"You belong to me now baby, you don't need to ever worry about anything anymore. You can tell me anything." His voice was so smooth and comforting. Deep inside of me, I felt a warm glow building up in my heart. It felt good to finally belong to someone.

When we arrived in Victoria, I was actually amazed at how small and quiet it seemed to be. The complete opposite of Vancouver. Before heading to the hotel, Mark wanted to drive down to stroll to check on his women and grab a bite to eat. He didn't like ferry food, so we skipped dinner on the boat. Stroll was only really about Ten blocks, all the girls out were dressed to the nines. They all had their hair and nails done and most rocking a killer tan. Some even seemed to have their own cars and such.

Robin said that since I was his new lady, I was special. I liked the way he draped his arm around my neck. I like being held in the crook of his arm. I was pleased to when I noticed some of the other girls giving me stare down glances. I had never been with a man like Robin. He made me feel so important and more than that, for the very first time, I felt truly safe!

Oh, how I wanted to please him. That night out for dinner I tried to order a shit ton of food. I wanted pasta and pizza, I was starving! Robin gave me a stern look. Somehow I realized he wanted me to take better care of myself and eat better. I changed my order as fast as I could to a salad and water. He nodded and rubbed my leg. I felt that warmth again in my belly. So did it matter if I was still hungry? At least Robin was happy with me.

After dinner, we drove straight to the hotel, he checked us in and once in the room, he sprawled all over the bed and turned on the TV. I couldn't seem to sit still. The bathroom was my favorite part of this room. It was huge and had fluffy white towels. The tub was huge too with jets. I could fit four of me in there. I found tiny bottles of bubble bath and shampoo and conditioner. It was so different from Rachel's bathroom that was ugly and small and smelled of piss. I decided at that moment, I loved it here. I wanted to stay in Victoria forever.

The next day Robin told me he was taking me shopping. I had come over from Vancouver with nothing. He wanted me to look good, he said. We walked through the crowded mall and went from store to store. Robin selecting every single item for me to try on. Each time I came out of a dressing room he would make me turn around slowly before deciding if it got added to the pile. When he told me how beautiful I looked that warm feeling in my belly got bigger and bigger.

There were so many beautiful clothes in the bags we carried and I was hoping he would let me pick out some comfy pajamas. But when Robin saw me looking at them, he slapped my hand, making me jump and almost fall back. "You sleep Naked from now on." He said, stepping up close rot me, his piercing eyes boring into mine. I nodded quickly and looked down at the floor. The last thing I wanted was for him to be angry and ruin our trip to the mall today.

Soon after, Robin started giving me instructions daily. He told me what to wear, how to do my hair and makeup, how to walk and even how to talk. If another man even tries to talk to you, don't look him in the face, understand?" He warned me, "Cause if you do, you're gonna be charged and I'm gonna have to pay cash money. And really I don't like other men talking to my women". He grabbed me and pulled me to his lap. I gazed into his eyes, trying to decide if he was pissed at me or not.

I didn't like it when he called me names but I did like being called his woman. It was confusing most times. He could make me feel so important one minute and then the next terrified and wanting to go home, wherever that was.

It was around that same time that I realized that Rachel and Pony had sold me to Robin for a drug debt and some extra cash. They had sold me out to a pimp and a serious one at that. He had a bunch of women who he took care of. In return, they used his name on the stroll and paid him a percentage of what they made nightly.

It was really hard to keep all the rules straight, Yet a part of me was excited to be a part of this new secret world, most knew nothing about. I liked the thought of a man taking care of me. For the first time in a long time, I again felt like part of a family. I finally felt like I was a part of something bigger than m. It was Robin and me against the world. I knew I owed everything to him.

That morning I woke up the loud pounding on my apartment door. I knew it wasn't the police as they announce themselves when they beat your door in. It was Robin; He was clearly released from jail in the early morning hours and didn't have his house keys to get in.

I jumped out of bed, in a panic, looking around the house quickly for Buffy. She had been there when I had finally gone to bed to pass out. She seemed to have left and not spent the night and I didn't have time to really think about it as Robin continued to scream in the hallway and beat my door in. I rushed over to unlock it.

I really didn't want to open that door, but I was terrified of him and knew what the punishment would be if I didn't. So I opened it. The first thing he did when he stepped into the apartment was hauled off and punch me in the stomach, it dropped me to the floor. " Don't you ever do that stupid shit again, ya hear me?" All I could do was stare at him. Too afraid to move or even give him a response. He headed to the kitchen to check the tin on the top of the fridge. He was checking his money. He had been in cells a couple days on some bogus charges or so he claimed. He was checking to see if I had the money there that was supposed to be waiting. He was pissed when he saw that it wasn't.

"What the hell Tanya, where is my money?"

I had worked a little since his arrest but not really. I had been tired and wanted to rest. I knew what would happen if I told him that, "I don't know what happened, it should all be there." Robin was standing in front of the mirror on the dresser, "Where the fuck is my Rolex?" He shouted.

"I don't know, you weren't wearing it? My mind was spinning. I couldn't think straight. That's when I remembered that Buffy had been to the apartment and spent the night. I ran out of the room and checked the coffee table and countertops, No Rolex! Fucking Buffy, she must have taken it, like Robin isn't going to notice his Rolex missing. I already told her no one ever gets to come here. "I don't know what you did with it," I said shaking and starting to cry. "I don't know, I swear, I don't know." Robin stood there for a few seconds, eyes locked on me. I could tell he was trying to decide if I was lying to him or not.

"Tanya, tell me where my fucking Rolex is and I won't be mad at ya." I knew better than that though. What was I going to tell him? I wasn't allowed to have people even know where we live, let alone in his house. Robin reached into the closet and grabbed a silver, wire coat hanger.

"Please, Please, Please Robin!" I screamed, "I don't know where it is, I don't know what happened to it." He drew back his arm and struck me hard across the back. He hit me again and again. He towered over me. Tears and snot streamed down my face and nack. "Please stop this Robin." I sobbed, "I'm so sorry." The more I begged for mercy, the more power he put behind his blows. I prayed at that moment that I would die, I prayed as I left my body again. After what seemed like hours, I was shaking uncontrollably and had pissed myself. Robin looked insane like he wasn't in his own head anymore. He didn't see me as that 17-year-old young girl.

He finally spoke to me in that voice and tone I had learned to fear so much. "You have one more chance to tell me before I kill you." I knew he was serious. I finally spoke, "Buffy, Buffy was here last night."

He was silent for a few minutes before he asked, "What the fuck was that crackhead doing here? Your asking for that junkie to steal from us."

Robin looked a little concerned about my back as he watched the blood pool around me, where I was seated on the floor. His voice suddenly changed. " Come here and let me see you. Jesus girl, you see what you make me do? You should have just told me that bitch was here." He pulled me from the floor and led me to the bathroom to clean me up. He lifted my shirt and touched my wounds. I flinched in pain.

Sometimes I can't help but feel like the devil is always out to get me. Every choice I make, every road I choose leads me to the wrong ending. A body and ending full of brokenness!

Every time Robin beat me, It was always the same scene as if scripted. It had never been like this before though. Only really slapping me around and punching me and shit when I disobeyed him or did not bring him home enough bank.

"Let's go, we are going to see your girlfriend."

Robin threw some clothes at me and once dressed, led me to the car. When we got to Buffy's hotel and stepped out of the car, Robin put his arm around me. I winced in pain, my skin was on fire.

Robin pounded on that hotel door. No one came but you could hear muffled noises from inside, Typical crack heads. " I know you're in there girl, I just want my shit," Robin yelled.

"Please Buffy, open up, he knows you were the only person at our place." I sobbed. Finally, I heard the deadbolt, then the door opened. "What do you want?" Buffy was standing in the doorway, clearly high as a kite. " I just want my Rolex, no harm, no foul." He said, " I know you have it."

"I don't have it, it's in a pawnshop on hastings." She said, tossing the pawn ticket at him.

"You better hope it's there or I'm coming back here." Robin Screamed, flashing his handgun in his waistband.

I never ever saw Buffy again.

STUPID JOHN

Three nights later, I was back at work. I was able to
cover up the bruises on my face with makeup, but the
scars and bruises over my back and the rest of my body
were much more difficult to hide, especially in this line
of work.

I was meeting a new client. A referral from one of my
regulars. "He's a great guy, you will like him," Andy
assured me. Against my better judgment, I allowed him
to pick me up and take me to a hotel. I never do that, I
always meet my dates at a few specific hotels. I don't
like getting into cars with anyone these days. I live with
so much fear and anxiety. Not getting into vehicles or
heading off to strange hotels keeps me in control of
where I'm going and where I'll end up.

He picked me up from the little coffee shop just down the street from my apartment. He was pleasant enough but quite on our way to the hotel. He didn't say much of anything and finally, when I noticed we were getting a bit far, I said, "Um, how much farther to the hotel?"

"We're not going to a hotel." He said.

"Where are we going?"

"To my place." He said.

"Um, I'm sorry, I don't go to clients houses. It's a strict rule and I'm surprised Andy never told you."

"You're a hooker, so why do you care where we do it? I'm not paying for you and a hotel.

"I'm sorry, but I said I don't go to clients houses, you can take me back to the coffee shop if you want, but I won't go to your house with you, I said politely.

"Well, I think you can make an exception, since, I'm such a good friend of Andy's," He said, glancing over at me.

"I don't make exceptions, Please take me back," I said nervously.

" I'm not taking you anywhere but my place, you will be fine."

"Look I'm sure you are a nice enough guy but…"

"Don't be so sure. I can be a nice guy but I don't really have to be, do I?" He said once again glancing at me. I was afraid of him now and I was really pissed for breaking my own rule. "Look, just stop the car and I'll get back, you don't have to bother…"

" Oh, I'm already bothered. I came all the way into the city to get you and I'm not taking you back until I'm done with you." He didn't seem angry when he said it, just very certain of himself. He spoke as if what-what he said was law and I had absolutely no say in the matter.

"Just stop please, this date is over!" I said harshly. I left no doubt that I had zero interest in continuing this with him any longer.

"I'll tell you when it's over!" He said, refusing to stop the car.

"Let me out!" I demanded and reached for the door handle, prepared to jump from the moving car. He beat me to it and I heard the doors lock. He stared straight ahead and didn't say a word. He just kept driving.

"Did you hear me?" I yelled again.

" Oh I heard you but I'm not stopping, we had a deal." He said softly.

"The deals off, let me out now!"

He kept staring straight ahead refusing to stop. I started to panic, but quickly realized it would do no good. I needed to keep my cool so I could think clearly. I had no idea what his intention was for me but I knew that they couldn't be good.

I noticed he kept his hand on the automatic lock button at all times. I was trapped. I knew his plans for me were not going to end in this car. He had a destination in mind and as we pulled into an expensive acreage neighborhood, I knew he had money. I knew from experience that people with a lot of money, know how to protect it! I knew I needed to make a run for it before I was trapped in his house.

He finally pulled into a driveway and opened his garage door. I prepared myself to fight the second the car stopped. I knew he would have to unlock the doors to get out of the car, so I was ready to bolt. But he was smart and waited to unlock the doors until the garage door was closed all the way. Almost like he had done this before. So cool, calm and collected! This left me doubting my chance for escape or even survival. However my survival instincts are keen and as usual, I was very aware of my surroundings. I knew I had to play it cool in order to get out of this mess, so I said, "Alright, you win, but only this once," I said in my softest, sweetest voice.

"I thought you would see it my way... Once you saw I was loaded, that is," He said, with no emotion, as if his fancy house made him more appealing to me. I shuddered at the thought but played along.

"Well it does look like a beautiful home," I smiled coyly at him.

"Yes it is, but don't get used to it. Once I'm done with you, I'm taking you back to what I'm sure is an old dingy apartment."

I ignored his comment and forced myself to calm down so I could think straight. I knew I wouldn't be able to fight him off, considering he was twice my size, so I was forced to use my wits. I also knew running was out of the question as soon as the garage door had closed behind us.

He unlocked his door and stepped out. My door was still locked. I sat there and waited, fidgeting in my seat. As he slowly made his way to my side of the car. I reached down and slipped off my six-inch stiletto heels. I knew I would have a better chance of escape on foot without those damn shoes.

He unlocked my door and offered me his hand. My hand was trembling but I took his anyway and stepped out of the car. I glanced around once more, desperate for an escape route but only found two doors: The garage door, which was closed. And the door that leads into the house, which I feared would be my demise.

I suddenly got an idea and said, " I need to grab my shoes." Before he could stop me, I was back into the car, slamming the door shut behind me and reaching for the garage door opener hanging on his visor. I then scrambled out of the drivers' side door. I heard him raise his voice, telling me to stop, then I saw him reach for the door opener on the wall. I was able to quickly roll under the door before it closed, leaving me safely on the outside and him, temporarily locked on the inside and scrambling to get out.

I heard him yelling now, but I wasted no time listening and instead ran towards the front gate, going to complete my escape. I felt relieved to be outside. I made it to the front gate just as I heard a car approaching behind me. I scaled the brick fence beside the gate easily but landed hard on my hands and knees. I knew I had to keep going, so as the gates opened and the headlights glared, I forced myself up and into a cluster of trees, trying to stay hidden from the headlights fast approaching.

I cowered under a tree, hoping the lights would rush right past me. I heard the car slow and stop. I heard footsteps, but I held my ground, trying not to make a sound. After a few minutes, the footsteps vanished and the car sped off, leaving me to breathe a sigh of relief. I sat there for a few minutes, trying to gather the strength to continue on foot. I quickly realized that I ached all over. I still hasn't healed from the beating Robin had given to me just days before.

After about fifteen minutes of feeling sorry for myself and resting my abused body, I knew I had to get up and get moving. But I also knew I would have to stay off the main roads. There was no way in hell I wanted to run into that crazed man again. I made my way through the trees and finally ended up on a narrow road. I was barefoot, limping and as I looked down, I am bleeding from two open cuts on my knees.

Finally, I found myself at the end of this long, windy driveway. I was cold, sore and exhausted but just couldn't bring myself to walk up that driveway and ask for help. I didn't know how far I had traveled and all I know is I wasn't going to last much longer. I hoped and prayed I would find somewhere safe and warm soon. I walked and I walked and I somehow managed to find myself back on another road that leads nowhere. I hurt so bad that each step makes me cry out in pain. I sat down on the side of the road, ready to just give up. I haven't felt this lost or alone in a long time, I curled up and tried to stay warm. I found myself missing Robin. "He may be abusive, possessive and my pimp, but at least I would be warm and somewhere safe," I told myself.

I lay there for what seemed like hours, but I really had no idea what time it was. We didn't have the cell phone back in the 90's. I'm not sure what got me moving again but finally, I was up and on my feet and walking again. I hoped this time at least back towards the city. I limped along slowly when I heard a car approaching. I instantly went cold, praying that bastard hadn't found me out here. It had actually been hours since I escaped him and he wouldn't be coming from that direction. I relaxed a little and hobbled on. The car pulled up beside me and slowed to a stop. I turned and looked in the window hoping to ask for directions.

"Are you ok?" A male voice asked. It was dark and I could only make out some of his features that shone from the street lights.

"Um yeah, I'm ok, just a little lost. Could you tell me how I would get back to the highway?"

"Where are you going?"

"Um, just into the city." I stammered, trying not to say too much.

"Well it's a long walk, I'll give you a ride."

"No!" I said loudly, certain that I did not want to get into another man's car.

"You're going to freeze out here. I'm not going to hurt you, I promise," His voice continued.

"Thanks but I really just need directions."

"Girl, it's about fourteen km's to the city, let me give you a ride. I really can't leave you out here, alone." "Fourteen km's?" My mind reeled, had I really walked that far?

"Look, just tell me where you live and I will drive you home, no strings attached. I'm not a stalker, I won't bother you, you will never see me again anyway." He grinned.

"Why do you care? I mean, I do appreciate the offer but you don't owe me anything. And well, I don't want to owe you anything. That never works out to well for me."

"You don't owe me anything. I told ya, no strings." He said, getting irritated with me.

It was cold and I wasn't about to make the walk fourteen km's and my spidery senses told me he was gonna be alright. I took the ride. We drove in silence for a while and he finally said, "So are you originally from here?. He smiled at me. He actually had a very nice smile and was his eyes were the kindest I had seen in a while. If I wasn't in this damn situation, I might have found this man attractive, but I had long since learned to not trust men, especially attractive ones.

"I, Ummm… I appreciate the ride, but I'm not really into chit-chat."

"Okay, fair enough. But, will you at least answer one question?" He asked, still grinned ear to ear at me. "Do you have a name?"

"Yes, I have a name."

"Well, what is it." He pushed, in a playful way.

"Tanya, my name is Tanya," I said. I thought about having him drop me a few blocks away from the apartment but as stretched out my leg and felt the throbbing pain,   realized I didn't have the strength to walk that far. "You can drop me off just past this next four-way stop, up there on the right."

He pulled his car up in front of my building and quickly jumped out and came around to open my door. He helped me out of the car. I seriously can't remember the last time a man opened a door for me or was kind, without wanting something in return. Without taking a piece of my soul. I took his hand and stood up on very shaky legs. I grimaced in pain but tried not to cry out.

He walked me to my building door. "Good night, take

care of yourself." He said.

"Goodnight," I said. " thanks so much again for the

ride." and closed the door. Grateful to be home,

Thankful to be alive.

I woke up to the apartment door opening at 6:30 AM.

I knew it had to be Robin. I still ache all over, my feet

barely being able to stand even the pressure of the

cotton sheet on my bed. I was in no mood for Robin this

morning and hoped he would just fucking go away.

Although I knew that wasn't going to happen.

"Hey, who's Ryan?" He shouted from the living

room. I ignored him, having no clue what the hell he

was even talking about. "Tanya, Who's Ryan?" He

asked, standing beside my bed now. "I give up, who's

Ryan?" I asked, rolling over onto my back to look him

in the eyes.

"That's what I'm asking you?"

"What! I don't know what the hell you are talking about." I said clearly irritated. "This, I'm talking about this, you dumb bitch!" He shouted and threw a piece of paper at me. It was a note that had been left on the front door of my building with his phone number. My heart stops, Robin now knows a man dropped me off here, at our apartment! And just after I was already schooled about people being here and knowing where we lived. I know what's coming, and so do you.

I leave my body again. I don't want to feel or remember the punishment that's coming!

"I need my money." I pulled my little black tank top over my head. The scent of the act, still lingering in the air. I gag at the thought of my shame. Most days I am able to go through the motions almost robotic. But this day, I couldn't help but feel like my price tag read "clearance, Damaged Goods."

"You're nothing." He said. Just another piece of my soul taken. "Pay you? You have got to be kidding, right? You weren't worth the time I spent away from my wife!" He threw my jean shorts at me. "Get dressed and get out, You little tramp!"

"I can't go back to my man without money." My voice cracking. Robin would not take this lightly. "He will kill me. Then he will come to kill you. He knows where I am, he dropped me off."

"I don't really give two shits what he does with you. I'm getting dressed and cleaned up and then I'm outta here. Make sure you're gone when I come out!" The bathroom door closed with a bang. I slipped my jean shorts over my hips.   That's when I noticed his wallet. I would pay myself, picking up his wallet quickly, I counted out what he owed me, nothing more. I placed the wallet back on the dresser and headed for the door. I grab my shoes and hear the water in the shower get turned off. As I open the hotel door to leave his hand reaches over my head and slams the door shut. His face twisted with rage.

"You little thief!" He grabbed my hands, forcing them open. The money I had taken spills out onto the floor. The color drains from my face. "Now you're going to pay, you stupid little bitch." He threw me up against the wall, hard. His fist crushing into my face, over and over; BLood slid over my tongue. Stars exploded before my eyes when he grabbed me by my hair and tossed me to the floor. He unleashed his rage on me. I screamed, yet no one came. I lay beaten and curled up on the disgusting floor of the cheap hotel. Unable to even find the strength to fight back. His breathing slowed and the door finally opened. That was my signal that he was finished with me.

"Now get out, before I throw you out!" With the last bit of energy I could muster,   crawled out of that room on my hands and knees. He locked it behind me. I pushed my body into a sitting position and leaned against the wall in the hallway to access the damage. I wiped the blood from my face with my tank top.

How had this happened?

I had forgotten the number one rule; Payment before pleasure. I would now face my man's wrath, showing up at home, no money and because bruises don't sell, I was fucked. I couldn't even try and turn a trick fast before heading back there, looking the way that I did. My best bet was to just get back to the apartment and face what I knew was sure to be coming.

I made it back to our apartment building but I could barely see the number fourteen on the elevator buttons. My right eye was swollen shut. As the elevator rose, so did my heartbeat. What was Robin going to do to me? I knew he definitely wouldn't offer me an ice pack for my wounds. I began to shiver, even though it was warm in the elevator.

When I walked through the door, Robin was talking on the phone. Kim, my wifey, stood in the doorway of the kitchen, trying to convince him to keep her there with him instead of sending her out on the stroll. I snuck to the bathroom, I dare turn on the light. A pounding drum had taken up residence in my head. I managed to get the water turned on and get undressed. I anticipated relief from the bath but instead, tiny needles penetrated my skin. I got out of the bath quickly, then pulled on a pair of my sweat pants that had been hanging on the back of the door. I had given up looking at myself in mirrors these days, except when applying my heavy makeup for work. Robin demanded I wear that heavy war paint night after night. My haircut and color wasn't the only thing to change since being sold to Robin. I was completely dead inside. All that remained was a shell of the young girl I was before.

Back in the living room, Robin was still on the phone. Kim was gone, probably off to make what mattered most to him..... Money. Robin would sell his own mother, given the right price tag. I walked out onto the fourteen-story patio for a smoke while Robin was distracted. Cigarettes had become just one of the coping mechanisms I had acquired. My hand trembled as I brought the cigarette to my lips. My heartbeat sounded like a jackhammer in my own ears. Robin was going to be so pissed at me.

As I flicked the smoke over the balcony, I shivered, Sensing Robin behind me. Time to pay the piper, I thought. I turned to him, his jaw dropped.

What the fuck happened to you?" I knew better than to pull away from him, but the sound of his voice sent my head spinning. "I asked the guy to pay me, but he said I was going to pay. He left his calling card on my face." My legs were shaking so hard, I didn't know if they would continue to hold me up. Robin got so violent when people fucked with his money. "He did this to you before you did the job?" He stepped back and started pacing. "No," I almost whispered. "When we got there he started moving fast. He said I was late getting there. I wasn't late, you know that you dropped me off. I didn't have time to get the money beforehand. I know I messed up. Please don't be mad at me, Please!" Robin didn't say another word, which scared me. My body trembled.

He stormed into the apartment, smacking the glass patio door on the way by. It cracked. He opens a cabinet in the kitchen, grabbing a couple handguns he had in there. He yelled towards the second bedroom, "Let's go Ranell! We have a fucking score to settle.

My heart raced as I looked over the city. Robin came up behind me again now. This time he grabbed me, no concern for any of my injuries and dangled my over the balcony, fourteen stories up. All I remember was screaming, " No! Robin, Please! Please don't drop me! I'm so sorry! I promise I won't ever do that again. I'll always get your money first. I promise. God, please don't let me fall!" I choked back the tears, " I promise Robin, Please!"

"Don't you ever show up after a job without my money! You hear me? If you do, I'll drop your ass off this balcony and you will be replaced before you even hit the ground, You got that, Bitch?!" I nodded and he let me fall into a heap on the balcony floor and stormed back inside the apartment. I sobbed uncontrollably as Robin yelled, "Let's Roll!".

I clung to the sliding glass doors for support as Ranell came into the room, pulling on his shirt. "What the hell?" He stared at me. "We ain't got time for this," Robin said, "We got a score to go settle." he tossed Ranell one of the handguns. "Some dirty trick did this and sent her home with no money. I'm gonna kill him. Don't nobody mess with my money!" He rushed out ahead of Ranell.

Ranell followed him with a quick glance back at me before the door closed.

I can't help but think that the devil is always out to get me. Every choice I make, every Road I take seems to lead me to the same ending. An ending full of brokeness.

REBELLION RISING

As the days and months passed I started to feel such resentment for him, This sense of rebellion was building inside of my soul. What could I do? I hated this man when he beat the shit out of me, and called me such vile names each and every day. But then it would feel good when he told me he loved me. He was always so happy when I gave him the money I made each night; I felt like I had accomplished something when I saw how proud he was of me when I brought home so much more than all the other girls. He always bragged to his boys how much game I had, how solid I was and how much money I brought in. Sometimes I truly believed the only reason he laid his hands on me was that I really needed the discipline, just like my father used to say! I was a bad girl, who didn't listen. Period.

Robin took care of me; He fed me, housed me, clothed me and truly made every single decision for me. Even down to my doctors' appointments and if they were important enough to attend. Life with Robin was almost impossible to think about and way too scary to imagine. I believed I had nothing without him, that I was nothing without him. He reminded me of this on a daily basis. Not that he needed to, I mean every night in this life, my life, was a reminder of the nothingness i felt. Every one of those hands that touched me seemed to be slowly rubbing me completely out of existence. I had been with so many strangers that as the time passed, the became just a blur of bodies, hands, dicks, and hundred dollar bills. Any slight act of kindness at all from a john was a shock and I always responded with disdain. I didn't trust anyone. I was nothing more than a worthless whore- Good for only one thing. I believed that no one other than Robin would love me, take care of me and accept my darkness. Robin pounded into my head that all of the "square" people hated me because of what i was doing. I thought of the look on my parents' faces should they ever know about this life, and I knew he was right.

***

I was always so desperate for a break, one night after being with Robin for about two years, although by that time it had felt like a lifetime, I tried to hide from him in the little apartment we were living in on the north side of the city. When I heard him slide the key into the lock I ran into the bedroom and hid in the closet, without really thinking. I suppose I thought he wouldn't be home long out that he wouldn't think to look in the closet and I could get a few hours of peace. Maybe I would be lucky enough to have one night without all those dirty old men pawing at me with their greedy, disgusting hands. Wanting the things i hated to give.

He walked past the kitchen and heard him coming for the bedroom. I slid down as low as I could in the closet and tried not to even take a breath. I heard him place his handgun on the dresser and unzip his pants. He sounded as if he was getting changed to head out. I held my breath and waited for him to leave. I heard him slide the dresser drawers shut and grab his watch from the night stand, but then slowly he pulled open the closet door, a terrifying smile came over his face as he stared down at me crouched on the floor. He must have heard my heart pounding out of my chest or the intense breathing that I was trying to hide.

"What the fuck are you doing, you stupid Bitch?" He asked in that low voice. I could see his tensed jawline pulsating with anger. When Robin used that voice and clenched his jaw, I knew to be terrified. The quieter he was the worse the beating that was coming would be.

"I'm tired," I said, hands already raised above my head to protect myself from the blows that I knew were coming. I started babbling, " sorry Robin. I just don't feel good, and I thought that if I laid down for a minute I would feel better."

"You dumb Bitch," He muttered as he grabbed me by the top of my head, his long fingernails digging into my scalp. He dragged me to my feet and slapped me hard in the face. The ringing in my ears was so loud from the blow, but I heard him say, "Just get to work, you dumb bitch." Then he pushed me out the door into the hall of our apartment building.

***

About a week or so later, I pulled a girl I knew on the stroll down into the alley behind the Old, grungy Empire hotel and asked her to help me.

"Come on Angie, just come with me for a sec." I grabbed her by the hand and hurried down the alley towards the dumpster, trying not to get seen by anyone.

"But why? Oh my God, if Ted finds out I'm not on the stroll, I'll be in Huge fucking trouble girl. Like fucking seriously, what the hell do you want."

At that time in the wee hours of the morning, the back alley behind the hotel is pretty much deserted. It was close to four in the morning.

" I need you to punch me in the face, like seriously, just do it." I stood close to her, looking into her eyes, willing her to hit me. I closed my eyes in anticipation of the blow. I could see our reflection in one of the windows from the hotel. As the sun was starting to rise, we were just two pretty, young, teenage girls, dressed almost the same in little tiny booty shorts and six-inch high heel shoes. If you didn't really look closely at us, you may not notice all of the makeup that didn't really seem to mask or cover up any of the fear, sadness, and loneliness in our eyes.

"What? Are you fucking crazy? Why the hell would I do that? You already had a black eye last week!' Angie backed away from me and started to walk away from me.

"No, Please wait!" I begged her. "Please just do this for me, I can't take it anymore and I want to go home. Tonight has been so dead and I haven't broken all night, I know I'm not going to make any money tonight. You know Robin, he is going to kick my ass. Maybe if I tell him a John robbed me, he will leave me alone tonight."

I seriously couldn't take the beatings from him anymore. The beatings came for a number of reasons, from not making his nightly quotas to breaking any of his numerous, ever-changing rules. I was tired, so fucking tired; I just wanted to go to sleep and never wake up. But I knew Robin was not gonna let me return home with Zero trap.

"Come on Angie. Like shit, Just do it, punch me in the face man, I won't be mad or anything, like for real. Just do this for me, Please!"

Angie frowned, balled up her fist and punched me in the face as hard as she could in the left eye. The face punch caught me off guard even though I had to beg her to do it. I almost fell to the ground in that dark alley. I held on to the cool surface of the dumpster and checked my face in the window. I could see the shiner under my left eye forming already. My skin was already turning blue and red all over the left side of my face, my eye swelling shut. I felt happy, felt relief. This would work.

"Thanks, girl, I owe ya, Big time!" I hurried out of the alley, a faint bit of hope in my heart as I held the left side of my face and jumped in a waiting taxi in front of the empire hotel.

I had it all planned out. I was going to tell Robin a date attacked and robbed me. That way I wouldn't be in any trouble when I returned back to the apartment empty-handed and battered. But Robin Laughed when I showed up at home and showed him my face. He rolled his eyes and laughed hysterically. " Is that all you got? You stupid bitch. YOU seriously think you can trick me?" He reached back and before I even had a chance to react or try to protect myself, he punched me in the side of my head, right above the temple of my other un bruised eye. He continued to laugh to laugh and mock me. "You want to be hurt? I'll show you pain Bitch!" His next blow to the back of my head now was much more painful.

"Please, Robin." I was trembling, fresh blood running down the side of my face and neck from a blown eardrum caused by the blow. "I'm so sorry, I promise I won't ever do that again, let me go back to work and make it up to you baby. I promise I'll bring back lots of money."

" You're such a little lying bitch, you know that." He said to me as he turned to walk into the other room. " You better you whore. The next time you lie to me, you know what will happen!" As he pointed to the closet.

And I did know.

THAT BLUE
LINE

Then came the day i walked into the little bathroom
at the Kindred House drop in center, Shaking so badly i
could hardly function. I pulled that little stick out of the
box that Athena had brought me from the drug store. I
took the test. I was pregnant.

My world in that moment started spinning in a haze
of desperation. I knew what this meant for me.

For several weeks I walked around in a daze, like a
shadow: Dark, hollow, flat. I was slowly imploding
under the weight of my choices. I had constant panic
attacks these days. Panic that caused me to claw at my
throat while gasping for air. I feared for my life and
now i feared for the life of my unborn child.

I wanted to run away but there was nowhere to go. Nowhere that reality would not find me. I couldn't escape. The one thing I had managed to avoid over the past 4 years was getting pregnant.

Robin had other children from a previous relationship that were being raised by family due to Robins lifestyle choices. Robin had been wanting to have another child for years now and not because he was a loving man and wanted to raise a family with me, but because he was wanting to fill a void left from the loss of the other children as well as have the ability to have complete control over me.

I remember telling everyone that day that i was going to die. That Robin was going to kill me.

The terror i felt having to tell Robin, I mean was the baby even ok? Robins rage had him blowing up and abusing me almost everyday now.

At my doctors appt a few weeks later, She could tell how i was feeling. Louis has known me now for many years and has had to nurse me through some bad dates and bad beating already in my young life. She is my person when it comes to anything health related. I know now that God placed that woman into my life to help me navigate through all the crazy stuff that had become my life. She was such a huge part of my survival looking back.

"Well Tanya, You're definitely pregnant," She said at my appointment I was finally able to book. I can still remember staring at the birth control poster on the wall in her office as i sat on the cold exam table and i just sobbed uncontrollably.

It had been four years since Robin had started talking about children. Four years I had managed to avoid my biggest fear- A Baby. Not just a baby, but his baby! Robin spoke of his other children often and it seemed to be the root of a lot of his rage. He would often go off on rants about what he would like to see happen to his family or what he would do to me if i ever tried to take his children like his family had done.

"One day Tanya, you are going to give me a child," He would say. I would laugh and pray in my mind. "Please Lord, don't let me get pregnant." Almost begging.

The whole time I was bonded to Robin in fear I was always thinking of a life free of him. When I look back at that time of my life, i felt like a caged animal, just wanting to escape and survive.

My pregnancy was honestly a complete blur. My mind did its best to protect me from that very painful time in my life. The whole time my belly grew, the violence increased, the beating more severe and I feared that I was soon going to die. We were living in some Dive motel on the west end of the city. Nothing was allowed to be spent on baby items. I was so terrified for her and for me. She always stayed so very still inside my belly, as if herself trying to stay hidden from the monster that was her father. I think back to that time now and i can't help but cry. I don't just cry for that twenty year old, broken young girl. I cry for that other little girl, the one who also did not ask for any of this. The one who was taught from the moment of conception to be silent, to go unnoticed. The anxiety she had to have felt and continues to feel throughout her life because of things she can't even remember. I cry for the scars left on her heart and soul that she didn't even know were there.

Things in the relationship shifted after getting pregnant and all Robin seemed to talk about was ways he could take my baby and end my life. I started telling everyone who would listen what I was afraid of, what I thought he was capable of. I was so disconnected now, feeling so empty and hollow inside. It was nearing the end for me, I could just feel it. It's the most eerie feeling knowing that you are going to die.

Robin had made me work the street all the way through my pregnancy. Not allowing me to stay home even one day when i wasn't feeling well. Which seemed to be most of the time. I went to every doctor's appointment alone and was terrified as her delivery date neared. Robin spent all of our money on drugs and booze and God knows what else as i worked, struggled and lived in motels.

A week before the baby was due Robins aunt had convinced him that we needed to go to her house and stay there while I had this baby. I loved this woman for that. She didn't know me at all but she knew what I needed. She knew what I was unable to make him understand and she saw the urgency! I am forever grateful for her in that moment.

The night I went in to labour Robins was drinking and was to drunk to even drive me to the hospital fifteen minutes away. Athena was the one to answer the call.

"It's time girl," I said into the phone.

"Are you sure?" Athena asked and I could already hear her getting out of bed, its was just after 1 AM. We exchanged a few words through contractions and she was headed to come and get me. Robin was still drinking when I left.

"Paul and I are just going to finish these beers," He slurred his words.

I prayed he didn't come.

Athena sped to the hospital. I knew she loved to drive like she was in a race car and these wee hours in the morning she proved it. It was February, It was cold and the roads were shit But she got me there, she was an angel. You know what else she was able to do? My dear friend Athena, She was able to actually have me feel something other than dread as i brought my daughter into the world. That day a little girl named Hope was born. And for the few moments that I got with her before he showed up, I was so deeply and madly in love with her.

He rushed in after meeting Athena in the waiting area. He paid no mind to me at all and just wanted to know where the baby was. Athena later told me that the first thing Robin asked when he arrived at the hospital, was if Hope was white or black. Athena was disgusted and didn't stay for very long once he arrived. Athena and I had been friends for a very long time. She was no stranger to my situation and she hated Robin and really had no problem letting him know that. The nurses however were swooning over Robin as he complimented them and worked his charm. Because of that charm, I didn't even get to fill out my babys live birth forms or any of that. All he allowed me to do was sign my name on them.

My heart sank when he came into the room with the forms in his hands. "I need you to sign these," He said as he took Hope from my arms.

I looked at the forms. "I want to call her Hope." I said. "And we aren't married Robin so we shouldn't give her your last name. My mom said that's a bad idea for tax purposes." I thought quickly. Robin didn't like to have any trail of our activity or anything like that so I thought that just might work. He hesitated.

"Nope, you don't get to make that decision. She is my daughter and will be named after me." And it was clear it wasn't happening any other way. In that moment, I lost everything! I lost my soul, my daughter and my will to live. That was the second time in my life I had thought about ending it all.

I had one night in the hospital with her, my little Hope. That sweet little girl that had survived so much already and she didn't even know it yet. I had one night before he changed everything. It wasn't just her name he changed. He changed our lives that next day when he took us from that hospital. To this day we are still trying desperately to recover from it.

THE END IS NEAR

My head was pounding as I attempted to peel myself up off the tile floor in our bathroom. I was in a complete daze, a dream-like state. I slowly reach around to touch the back of my head and I could already feel the almost golf ball sized, painful lump that was forming there.

I looked at my fingers after touching the lump, no blood. This time. Good, I thought as I let out a sigh of relief. My whole body ached. Gently, I used my hands to prop myself up as I attempt to stand. I reached my feet and wandered carefully and quietly from the bathroom, through the kitchen and I observed the mess we had left behind in the living room. The coffee table is off center and a piece of the glass is smashed out of it and all over the floor. His black Adidas zip-up hoodie was in a heap on the floor too. I took a moment to appreciate the long breaths of air i was able to freely take in now that his hands were no longer wrapped tightly around my throat, slowly choking the life out of me.

Hesitantly, I peak out of the patio door just off the kitchen. I notice him sitting down slumped in one of the deck chairs. He raised a cigarette to his lips and took a long, deliberate drag. As he exhaled slowly, he dropped his head into his hands. His rage appeared to have subsided for a brief moment.

Another lump starts to form, this time in my throat. I tried to choke back the tears as I swallowed hard. I shakily leaned my tired and sore body against the cool counter top and stood there watching him. To me, it felt like an eternity, but it was probably only a few minutes. A thousand thoughts, a thousand memories, flashed through my mind. I didn't know how I was going to escape this house today. Looking at the clock on the stove and it reads 8:42 AM. We are already over 14 hours into this battle and I know it's not over yet. Where is the phone? I look around the room quickly, desperately. Nothing.

We had been in this place hundreds of times before, and I mean hundreds of times. The place he would hurt me, the place where he would want me to beg for my life over and over. So why was this time different? It was different because it was the first time I had ever actually realized that he would ultimately kill me. And now we shared this small child together. A child who he was so attached to, her barely let me near her. Which is the opposite of what most expected from him. But after she was born it was as if i had become the plague. He saw how much she wanted and needed me and that made it even more important that he keep her from me. He kept telling everyone how much he loved her and yet the damage he was causing by not letting her bond with me was irreversible.

This was day two of his rage. The baby must have been asleep. She had begged for me last night while he beat me. She is so small and yet has seen and heard so much already in her young life. The more she wants me, the more enraged Robin becomes. I wish I could be strong enough for her, for myself. Today may just be the day he ends it all. I want to go home to my mom. Every single time my life feels threatened, i want my mother. Or at least the idea of a mother, someone to protect me and keep me safe. I'm just so tired these days, so much misery and fear. It fills my soul. I long for peace, I long for protection, but it never comes.

It's been a few months now since we have had our baby and I have been working every single day & night. Im home long enough to sleep and shower and maybe get the house clean. Robin doesnt allow me to spend any time with our daughter and in fact these days he has me sleeping on a piece of foam on the floor in the spare room. Robin sleeps with the baby in teh master bedroom. The door locked. He feeds her and bathes her and cares for her. I am not allowed to even really touch her and as I write this I can't help but be filled with such rage for my 21 year old self. How could I have allowed this man to have such power over me? And then I think about that little girl and Im so angry for her, for what was taken from her.

Robin came through the patio door and spotted me in the kitchen. He didn't even take a moment or hesitate. He ran and tackled me like a football player, his hands around my neck. We fell to the floor and I think I passed out or was knocked out on the tile floor.

When I come to, Robin had me seated in the chair at the kitchen table. There is blood running down my face from the side of my head that I smacked on the floor in the fall. As I try to get my bearings and figure out what is going on, Robin grabs my hair and pulls back my head. The look on his face, I will never forget! In the five years we had been together, I had never seen him look so empty. As if his soul was gone and all was left was his darkness.

"You see this fucking paper? You are going to write a letter to me," He screamed. He had clearly continued to drink and get high while I was knocked out on our bathroom floor earlier. "You are going to give me all the parental rights for Robyn, You got that?"

I began to whimper, my thoughts racing. He was going to take my daughter and take my life. Had I told the right people? Had I told enough people? I knew this day had been coming.

"You are going to tell everyone you can't take care of her, that you are a whore and a drug addict! Got it!" As he pushed my face down into the paper on the kitchen table. I was trembling as I began to write the words he repeated over and over.

Even though I was completely terrified in that moment, I was still able to think about the room as a crime scene. A bonus for being on the street for so long I guess. I was attempting to leave evidence all over the house since the fighting had began the night before. I had already ensured Robins DNA under my fingernails when i clawed at him while he choked me out on the bathroom floor. The same place in which i had laid unconscious for hours. There was blood dripped on the tile in the kitchen as well and now I was shaking so uncontrollably that it made it easy to leave pieces of paper crumpled on the floor for the police to find later due to making mistakes. Robin wanted clear neat handwriting so that it didn't look like i had been forced to write this letter in any way.

I'm not sure how long he had me sit at that table that day. But the fighting and beating lasted ALL day! He had me cook dinner for him and his friend. They sat in the living room, playing video games, smoking weed and drinking beers. Every so often he would come to where I was. In the kitchen preparing dinner, he came in and punched me in the face and the back of the head, blood poured on the floor as my teeth busted through my lip. He had grabbed a knife off the counter and cut my shirt off of me. I wasn't allowed to get changed or put on more clothing. I remember hearing the baby cry and I had attempted to go and get her.

Sometimes if Robin got drunk enough he would let me and I could care for her, I would get my chance to love on her a little before he would realise he had let his guard down. Not only was she longing for me but I was slowly slipping away the longer he kept her from me. To be kept from mothering your child when you are in the same room. When she cried, my breasts still leaked for her months after she was born, even though I had never been allowed to breast feed her once we had left the hospital.

I attempted to climb the stairs to his bedroom where she was laying and as I hit the top step I felt his hands wrap into my hair as he pulled me back. My feet slipping out from under me, I feel my guts go. I tumbled down the stairs to the floor below. He smiles down at me from the top of the stairs. "Don't touch my daughter you stupid bitch, you signed your rights away remember." He yelled as he grabbed the phone he had been carrying. Our daughter was screaming now from the bedroom and there was nothing i could do for her. I wanted to die. He called our cab driver. "Bobby, come get this Bitch." He yelled into the phone. I could hear Bobby on the end of line saying he had a fare and would be 20 minutes. Bobby had gotten several calls through out the night last night too and each time he would show up and Robin would refuse to let me leave. Bobby has known me a long time and I could tell by the look on his face each time he arrived that he wanted to help me but didn't know how.

For the next 20 minutes Robin continued to beat me while we waited for the cab driver. He had gone and gotten the baby from upstairs. "Take a good look you dumb whore, you are never going to see her again. You hear me?" He screamed. I nodded in agreement, just wanting this all to stop. My body was shaking uncontrollably now. With the baby in his arms he reaches over and smashed my head into the wall next to where i was sitting. The baby screams louder so he smashes my head again. All i can do is close my eyes and pray that Bobby gets here soon. I see headlights, It's Bobby. I prayed that this time Robin would let me leave. The longer im held here, the more I fear I may not survive the night.

Bobby knocks on the door and Robin lays the baby on the floor in the living room. He grabs me by the top of the head and drags me to my feet. He punches and kicks me all the way to the door. I have had all of my clothes cut off of me at this point and am in a little t-shirt and a pair of panties. The door opens and Robins tosses me out at Bobby. "Take this Bitch and dont bring her back here." I collapse in Bobby's arms as he carries me to the parking lot and his waiting taxi.

"Why did he do this to you Tanya? We need to take you to the police," He said as he started his car and sped out of the parking lot. Afraid Robin would chase him, no doubt.

"Take me downtown Bobby." I sobbed as I tried to straighten out what little clothing I had on. It was early in the morning and I knew I could get a room at the hotel downtown. I needed to wash up and clean my wounds and figure out my next move.

For three full days I stayed in the hotel and nursed
myself back to health. I didn't notice just how bad I had
been beaten until I arrived downtown. Here I was this
frightened twenty-one-year old girl, beaten to a pulp
and no one to call to help her. Robin had stripped me of
everything. I was a shell of a person now, left with
nothing.

Three days in however, I felt stronger and was ready
to start making some phone calls. I had been calling
Robin for two full days and no one was answering.
First thing I needed was housing. I picked up the phone
that was on the night stand and I called Maureen. This
woman was an amazing outreach worker who worked
for crossroads and always was offering me services and
ensuring I had her card. She had even come by the
house on a few occasions to drop off stuff for the baby.

She had known me now for several years and even though we didn't talk much about my home situation she wasn't stupid.

"Crossroads, Maureen speaking." She said into the phone as she picked up. I could barely get the words out, "Maureen its Tanya." I sobbed. "Im at the Empire Hotel and I need help." The crying is uncontrollable now. It's the first time I have really cried since the beating had started at my house nights earlier. Reality has started to set in that he has my daughter.

"Stay right there, don't you move, Im on my way." Maureen says into the phone as I sob. Fear is rising in my throat. How am I going to explain my wounds and battle scars? How am I going to get my baby a way from him?

Thirty minutes later and Maureen is standing in the doorway to my hotel room. I try and look relaxed and have done my best to cover my face. The same face that had been a punching bag just days earlier and I start to tell her what has happened. After I tell her everything she hugs me tight and picks up her phone and make the calls to ensure I have a bed at the safe house. She also puts a call in to Jo-Ann at vice. "Tanya, we need to file a report with the police. Its important as he has the baby." She touches my leg gently, looking me in the eyes. I nod and she again grabs her phone.

This call was even harder to listen to as I know this is what is going to seal my fate if they are not able to catch him and protect me. Maureen speaks on her phone for a few minutes and then returns to my room. "Grab your stuff Tan, youre coming with me to the house and Jo is heading to your townhouse to see if Robin is home," She said. I grab my bag and we head for her car outside. The drive to the house is quiet. Im terrified of what is going to happen when Vice get to my house. Robin is going to be so pissed at me. I then remember the letter. I quickly tell Maureen everything as we head to the house to get my intake all completed.

She nods her head and listens so patiently. "Don't worry Tanya, we will get him." She reaches over and squeezes my hand.

Within an hour Vice is calling Maureen back to inform her that they have been to my place and that there is no one there. They are needing permission to enter and search the premises. Maureen loads me back in the car and we head to my house on the west end of the city. Its been several days since I've been there.

Pulling up I can see Ed and Jo standing in my parking lot with my landlord. They are needing to gain entry as I clearly don't have keys to the residence any longer. The landlord greets me and appears very concerned with all of the police presence. He slips the key in the lock, unlocks the dead bolt and heads back to the office. We enter the house to find everything destroyed. Robin has trashed the townhouse and removed anything of any value. All of my clothing and belongings are cut up and left all over the floors of the townhouse. Robin is gone, My baby is Gone! I cant help but fall to the floor and cry.

How am I going to win against him? How am I going to get my baby back?

***

Days quickly turn into months and the police had yet
to locate Robin or my little girl. My supports have
helped me with housing as well as funding for school. I
have reached out to my mother now and all she did
was accuse me of ruining my daughters life and
lectured me about the police involvement. Not once did
she offer any real solid advice or support. I don't know
why I kept hoping she would do right by me, that she
would decide one day I was worth it and that she loved
me enough to fight for my life and the life of my
daughter.

Vice well, they haven't really done a damn thing since
the day we walked through my town house and I
charged Robin with Human Trafficking and aggravated
assault. In the years I have spent living this life on the
street, I had heard the police were not all that great at
helping girls escape their Pimps or getting charges to
stick. I mean I had watched so many girls die in this life
or lose their own sanity. It was rare, if ever girls were

able to get out and if they did, we certainly didnt see them again to hear about it.

This is the first time in years I have been off the street for any good length of time. Im starting to feel like maybe I can do this, starting to feel normal. Something I was unsure I would ever feel again. The fear is starting to subside a little too, the more I talk to professionals and work through my toxic bond to my abuser, the stronger I feel.

My house phone rings, Its late at night and im hesitant to even answer. I know that the only people with this number are my support so i relax a little and reach for the phone. "Hello." I said.

"Tanya, Its Kate, They found Robin," She sounded a bit panicked as she told me that she was on her way to pick me up and that we would be traveling a couple hours north of the city. Robin had apparently been picked up for some assault and was brought in due to his outstanding warrants for pimping and the assault on me.

"Where is my baby?" I asked before she could even finish letting me know what the plans were.

"She is there at the police station with the officers, be sure to have a copy of your court order, they are going to need it." She said. "See you in twenty minutes, this is great news honey." Although I didn't feel all that great about it. I was excited and relieved that had found my little girl but something just seemed off to me.

We sped down the highway and I remained silent most of the way. Praying that he was locked in a cell and I would not have to see him at all. I couldnt bare that. Now im here taking his daughter. He always told me he would kill me if i was to do that. The little bit of stregth I have grown in the past couple of months starts to slip away as the fear rises in my guts and the realization of what is about to happen settles in. I quietly sob in my seat the rest of the drive.

As we pulled into the parking lot at the police station my anxiety begins to rise. "He is going to kill me Kate." I said.

"Don't worry Tanya, you are safe. We are at the police station. He cant do anything to you." She tried to reassure me but even her tone was a little uneasy too. Walking through the doors, I had anticipated seeing an officer with my baby and rushed to the front reception desk, hopeful she was there. As I ran up on the desk a part of my heart sank. There he was, Laughing with the cops, our daughter on his lap. The female officer spotted me and jumped up right away meeting me at the desk.

"You must be Kate," She said looking at Kate and not really acknowledging me. I was used to that kind of treatment though. Robin always had a way of making me look like the bad guy. "I will need a copy of the parenting order." She said as Kate handed her the envelope with all of the information. "Robin, you have to give her to them." She said as she took a copy of the order for her records.

Robin stood from his seated position, our daughter reaching for me as soon as she sees me. "Mama, mama." She is babbling as he picks up her bag of belongings. Robin brings her to the desk and hands her off to me. The rage in his eyes tell me everything I need to know about my future. He is not going to let me get away with this. I can put my life on it.

We head back to the city and back to my little apartment. I am so over filled with joy to have my baby back and yet terrified of what this all will mean. I want my mom. She still never comes. And to this day never has.

Its only a couple of days and Robin is released from jail. No bail required and no Protection order to help my daughter and I. Its not long before he knows where I am living and he starts to come by my house wanting to see "his" daughter. I phone the police and am told that I can not deny him access to our little girl.

The weeks that roll out ahead are intense to say the least. Robin is at my house almost daily now wanting to see my daughter. Im too afraid to terll him any different. He forces his way into my home and helps himself to my money and anything of value that he can sell for drugs. "Remember, I own you." He says as he continues to take what's mine.

I live in fear each and every day now. Not the same fear as when I was on the street, this is a different fear. I cant even begin to explain the uneasy feeling it leaves in my soul. Even my supports are starting to fall to the way side as i dont live in the program and they have others they need to help that are there and in crisis.

Again I am living in shame and fear and not telling anyone.

Is this really my life?

The last day Robin stepped foot in that apartment he had come to pick up our daughter and asked to keep her an extra night. I had started to grab her diaper bag and decline and he attacked me from behind.

I saw stars as my head was slammed against the cement walls of the apartment. He was foaming at the mouth and all of the humanity had left his eyes. As he began to choke me out on the floor he said, "Im taking her now and you are going to let me." He said, so calm my heart almost stopped. That calmness that came over him, I can still see that scene today as if it was happening right now.

I was done. I was tapped out. I was tired and alone. He had won. He had everyone on his side. I was nothing to no one and there was nothing I could do to change that.

As I sat bleeding and sobbing on the hallway floor, Robin packed up that little girl and promised her she would never lay eyes on me again. As he waved at me, so did she. My heart and spirit broke right then and there! Never was it fully repaired.

I was failed by the parents who were supposed to protect me. I was failed by the police force that was suppose to help me. I was failed by myself for not having it in me to fight any longer.

I vowed to NEVER be in a situation like this again, To never allow any man to have control over my life like this ever again! If others were not going to help me find my strength then I would do it on my own.

And I did!

COMPLETE
360

I walked into the office at 3:45 PM, a young girl was completing her intake with Liz, a support worker. I said hello and heading for the log book. Shift change would happen once this intake was complete.

"Did you used to have red hair?" The young girl asks. It takes me a few seconds to even register that she is talking to me.

"I did, a long time ago," I said. "Do I know you?

"I'm Star, I've been gone to Vegas for a while. I was with Angie. Not anymore, I'm trying to get my shit together." She said.

Now, Angie, I remembered. She and I had worked the same stroll for years together. We got along alright but our Men were always in competition to see who would have the most girls on the stroll. It was annoying and would sometimes have Angie and I Beefing for shit that had nothing to do with us. I laugh now at the memory.

"Oh ya girl, I remember you. You're in the right place to get your shit together." I head for the stairs. Leaving Liz to finish up Stas intake so that she can finish up and end her shift. There are a few girls upstairs watching tv, waiting for dinner.

"Tan, You're here tonight?" Mona screams with excitement.

"Yes Ma'am, I sure am so no Bullshit tonight miss." I laughed and head for the kitchen to get dinner started. Looks like Spaghetti it is tonight. I'm so glad these girls are finally getting the hang of meal planning and setting things out for me the night before. Teaching them life skills has actually been a ton of fun. I mean I remember not knowing how to do any of this either. We have been teaching them all about budgeting and saving their money.

I grab a pan from the cupboard and start dinner. Mona has joined me and begins to set the table. " How many plates do we need? Mona Asks. "is that new girl staying?"
Her name is Star and I would set her a plate. It's her first night, so go easy on her." I laughed and continued to cook.

Mona has been in and out of this safe house several times over the past year and we have all grown attached to her. It's hard not to, her laugh is infectious and her spirit always lifts me. I am always so grateful to see her and spend time with her when she comes and stays with us.

"Something smells amazing!" Chrissy slams the front door. "Yay, Tanya, you're here tonight? How long until dinner is ready, I'm starving," she said.

"Shouldn't be much longer, go and get washed up. And can you please knock on the office door and let Liz and the new intake, Star know that dinner is almost ready." I said, as I finished off the Caesar salad and tossed garlic bread into a basket and placed it on the table.

10 minutes later, 6 half-starved girls and Liz and I are sharing a meal and chatting about our day. Mona is celebrating today. She has 60 days clean, the intense day program that we got her into has been helping keep her on track this time. I couldn't be more proud of her.

"Sixty days, Bitches!" SHe yells with excitement as she tosses me her 60-day chip. A couple of times already this year Mona had almost died from heroin overdoses. She has been using more these days. No doubt to numb the pain of the shit she's been dealing with. Over the last 12 months, several of her friends have overdosed on drugs or been murdered and dumped by someone who is targeting them. It's a scary time for these girls. We are working with Mona every day to help her overcome her addiction and work through some of her painful past.

Star is very quiet and doesn't say much at dinner. The first couple of nights are always the hardest. Mona offers to help her get settled into a room, while Chrissy and the other girls clean the kitchen and Liz and I complete shift change.

An hour later, Mona and the others are all sitting in the living room, laughing and trying to choose a movie they can all agree on. I run to the kitchen and throw some popcorn in the microwave. We never watch movies around here without popcorn, covered in butter and white cheddar popcorn seasoning. As the smell of popcorn fills the room, I hear Star.

"Where are the staff in this place?" She asks, almost as if she thinks there is no staff on site. I quickly peek my head around the corner and jingle the keys that are attached to the lay around my neck. "Star, hunny, I am the staff," I say with a chuckle.

"You work here? Damn girl, I thought you lived here too!" I came and sat beside her and we laughed and laughed.

"Star, you see, if I can change my life and escape this bullshit so can you." We spent the rest of the night talking about our dreams. The girls seem to really show their true selves when we spend time dreaming and getting them to think outside of this little box they have been cornered into.

In those moments, with these girls, it's so clear that we are all just wanting the same thing: Love and acceptance. It didn't matter if we were still in the trenches of the street life or working our way through the wreckage that was once our life. We all wanted the same thing.

I take a moment, I'm grateful and my heart so full. Here I am just a few short years later and I'm sitting in this same house that saved me, pouring into women just like me, women that for the most part have been written off by society and feel completely alone. I give them HOPE. It's hard to see light at the end of any tunnel when you are surrounded by dicks, death, drugs, and despair. My life had come Full Circle.

Tonight at Eleven, we have a Shocking story of
several Canadian teens have been victims of Human
Trafficking, sold for sex by predators.

Hearing those words woke me out of my half sleepy
daze as I lay in my bed. I grabbed the remote, turned
up the volume and sat in almost a trance-like state,
staring at the television, listening to each and every
word the man on the news said.

He began by explaining these predators were preying
on young girls, telling them all the things that they
wanted to hear, making them feel loved. Making them
believe they were their boyfriends. The women
involved would befriend the young girls, making them
feel important and special. Then these men and women

would manipulate these girls into selling their bodies and souls. Some of these girls were recruited from high schools and malls; others were found at bus stops and now even more on line on those popular social media platforms that we all use a little too often. It sounded all too familiar to me.

One of the things that shocked me the most was how young these girls seemed to be. I mean I know I was thirteen when I was taken to that treatment center in Burnaby and met Rachel, but it really never hit before just how young I was. I remember in the beginning years in the game being sold to a serious pimp and being scared out of my mind. How I had believed Robin when he told me he wasn't like the others- that he loved me and that he would protect me. The girls on the news that night had been told a lot of the same things. Being manipulated and brainwashed in the same way I had experienced so many years before.

So many feelings washed over me as I listened to the news; So much sadness for those young girls, So full of anger for what they had to endure and all they had survived. I was shocked this was still happening to so many others, and then a sudden feeling of validation came over me. I mean most of my life, I have believed I needed to keep those early missing years of my life a shameful secret from the rest of the world. So many years I truly believed that all of the bad things that had happened to me in my life had been my fault. Now in that moment late at night. As the news played it was if the blinders were taken off. In that very moment, I began to see the truth; I'd been the God Damn victim! What I had been was a walking target. I had been trafficked, sold and placed into sexual slavery and now I finally had a name for it. For decades I called myself a survivor but was unable to put into words what I was a survivor of. Was it Prostitution? Was it Domestic Violence? Was it the system? I could never really put a name to it.

Now that I knew how to identify what had happened to me. I had been such a damaged young girl, damaged but not stupid. I had wanted so badly to be accepted and loved by someone, anyone back then. Rachel, Pony, and Robin had all said all the right things to me, I had believed them, but it was all a lie. For the first time, I began to feel so much anger towards the people who had exploited me, rather than continue to be angry at myself for all the wrong turns, all the huge mistakes! There was such a sense of forgiveness to myself that washed over me. It was like someone had finally washed away all of the pain, all of the sin.

For as long as I can remember I had been so wrapped up in my own survival, but something in my mind and heart shifted that night as I watched the newscast. I wanted so badly to reach out and hug each one of those young girls and remind them of their beauty and their worth. I wanted to tell them how worthy they were of real love and that the life they thought they knew was all a lie that would change them forever. I wanted them to know that I understood their pain- as it was my pain for so long, many years ago. That I too knew what it was like to feel unloved. I just wanted to help them all. Just like I had been, these young girls were being beaten, abused and forced to sell their bodies to the highest bidder. I wanted at that moment, for the very first time to share my story. I mean really share it. Not the sugar coated version I had shared for so many years but My real story. The good, the bad and the ugly.

That evening started me on a path that is sure to become such a very important part of my life. A real epiphany of sorts. I began to dive into the still ongoing issues that are Trafficking in Canada and Decided I was done being silenced. I mean I had been in the shadows, hiding my truth for almost two decades. I began blogging and working on my book outline. I also began to get very loud on social media about this Human Trafficking issue. There is such power in sharing your story. Something happens when you bring your darkness into the light.

I knew I wanted to do more. I knew that the girls on the news that night were not the only ones who were in need of help. There were definitely other girls like them, girls like I had been the summer I ran away from home at thirteen. I wanted to ensure others understood Human trafficking and what it is doing to children around our country.

***

Why didn't you leave? Why did you stay for so long? Didn't you want to leave? These were just some of the questions I was asked when I started to share my story with others.

I thought carefully about how I should answer those questions and share something that for me was s hard to put into words. I myself have only just begun to fully understand my connection to Robin and why I stayed for so many years. I wanted others to understand too, especially my daughters.

When I first had read about Stockholm syndrome, I thought that was just a term used for victims of war or kidnaping survivors. But I have come to learn that pimps and predators like Robin use the age-old trick of trauma bonding to take full advantage of their victims. First, they are nice- I mean, really, really, nice- to a young, already very damaged girl; take her to a fancy dinner, buy her clothes and listen to her problems. Then soon after, beat her up, but just a little, when she misbehaves and steps out of line needing discipline. Then again lay on all that shit about "I love you." with another smack to the back of the head or a push down the stairs. These vile people know that if they apply the right amount of what looks and feels like love and affection and then toss in some moments of violence, they will have constructed the perfect slave. A commodity that will obey them and their every word.

And that is just what the victims are to these pimps and predators; a commodity, nothing more. What's sad is that for so many years I didn't realize I was just a dollar sign; I mean at that moment, I believed I was being protected, loved and disciplined!

I hadn't even known I was a victim. "At first I thought it was all my idea, everything from being out on the street to not having the courage to leave," I said. It's only now that I see that the way I was manipulated and programmed by Robin caused me to bond with him. What was happening to me during that time, happens to all other young victims. Human trafficking becomes this very complicated mental process. I believed for years that Robin was taking care of me. He knew that and used it against me to do what he wanted. I would have done anything for that man.

A couple of years ago when I started to speak my truth a little and talking more and more about my past I realized that I still had a lot of the same fear I had years before. I mean even though I knew I was safe from him. Deep down inside a part of me wanted closure- to let go of all of that fear that had consumed my mind and heart for so long. To finally let go of the pain and shame from all those years so long ago.

The day I saw him again I remember being so stunned. I remembered Robin as this monstrous man. This man that towered over me, causing pain to my flesh and wounds to my soul. It started to make sense to me. I mean, of course, I viewed Rob as Larger than Life, God-like man! He had manipulated my mind, abused my body and exploited the young girl I was. With every single blow I took and the name he called me, he seemed to grow in height and size in my troubled, abused mind.

As I began to work through all of what had happened to me in my life, the fear, pain, and trauma that Robin had caused in my mind, heart and soul. I finally after two decades saw him for what he was- A small, sad, deformed person. No longer a monster in my nightmares, no longer a man to fear. I actually felt a bit of sadness for him.

Both Pony and Robin were able to abuse and exploit me because I was not missed by anyone. You would think people would have taken notice, but not a soul did. That someone would have missed me enough, but they didn't. That they would wonder if I was alive and what had happened to me, but they didn't. Maybe file a missing person report, but they didn't. For that little girl, None of that happened. I knew I was all alone without anyone to fight for me. I was just another kid in the system, another young girl with daddy issues. So they took me. It was if no crime was ever committed by these people. There seemed to be only air left behind and no one really noticed. I still can't help but think, "How clever of them."

To target the ones who are unloved and alone. The ones that are so broken and so desperate for love, they will take scraps. The ones in care and forgotten about. On so many different occasions during my time trapped in this life, Parents would approach me with pictures of their children, desperate to find them and take them home. I would often think, "Wow, where are my parents? Why haven't they even bothered to try and find me?" Just another message sent to my soul that I was unwanted and worthless!

It was those messages and feeling of aloneness that kept me a Prisoner for so long. Trapped for much longer than my time on the street. I was stuck in my own head, hiding the shame in the shadows.

***

Do you even know my name?

Do you even see me?

To all of the men that used me each night, I was not a woman. In fact, I was not even a human being. I was just a few bills in their pockets. To feel and know this as a young teenage girl, during those most important years that define our self-worth and identity, proved to be devastating. I mean how is a young girl supposed to process this? To feel and know that so many men didn't care about me. In fact, most celebrated my humiliation and pain. That was probably the biggest wound to my soul.

This awareness left me to lose all love, even for myself. When others don't value and love us, it becomes so hard to love ourselves. Shame embarrassment and guilt fill the gaping hole in our hearts where love should be. We all know that the brain and the heart don't always agree. My heart was so wounded- wounds left by all of the men that treated me as if I was worthless. There are places to this day or smells and songs on the radio that trigger the memories.

As I prepare to press print and publish my story, to bare my soul for the world to read, I feel my heart pounding in my chest. I can smell my sweat and feel my anxiety rising in my throat. But I am still here, I am still alive!

I remember what Robin always told me, what he for years had essentially beat into my mind. How he would keep telling me that I must never trust anyone and never say a word about life and all the rules. How I should never give my real name or age or ever try and explain what we did. How I must always keep my mouth shut. How I must never tell anyone our truths!

It was in that moment, I chose to tell, I will tell my truth and I will tell it to everyone who will listen. I choose to no longer be silent. I am no longer afraid of those demons. I am no longer afraid of him, he no longer has any control over me and he never will again!!

So I talk, I tell and I talk some more. From the very beginning, even from the very first memory of abuse in my childhood home when I was so little. I talk about how I suffered and lived for many years in complete fear. I talk about being so confused as a young girl and only want to feel loved, to feel as if someone wanted me.

For those of you wondering what happened to our little girl we shared together, We reconnected when she was 17 after nearly 13 years separated and even though our relationship is complicated and hard sometimes to work through, we are working through it! He didn't win. He didn't get to keep her from me forever. He was only able to keep me in the shadows for a little while.

The words throughout this book flowed out onto this paper and I am really unsure how others are going to react to what is all in these pages; but when I see so many words of encouragement and how so many women are excited to read my story, to bring light to my darkness! It's those words, messages and phone calls that make my heart truly soar. I feel the strongest I have ever felt and for that, I am truly grateful.

I know for a fact he lied to me, I am the Strong one! I am in control of My Life!

And understand now, really understand; I am no longer hiding my past in the shadows. I am a strong woman, with an even stronger voice and spirit, a voice that will protect others from the same fate as me and so many other women right here in Canada.

I Spent so 22 years of my life shackled by shame. I had always felt it. It had been apart of my life since my earliest memories.

I felt it when i was rejected. When i was made to feel unworthy and of absolutely no value to anyone.

I felt it when i was raped and couldn't tell anyone. Believing for so long it was all my fault.

I felt it when i tried to hide who i was, apologize for who i was and minimize my talents.

Have you felt it? If you are human, i bet that you have- the result is always the same. Shame makes us feel small, flawed and certainly not good enough. Shame is fear of being unworthy and it adversely affects our relationship with God, ourselves and others around us. It greatly hinders our ability to receive God's unconditional love and share it with others.

Because of God's great love, I began to really discover the power in God's word to break through all the lies. Breaking free from the shackles of shame is not something that happens over night or in a quick fix ten step program. It is however a grand, ongoing adventure of discovering the depths of God's power to transform us, recreate us and continually renew our souls.

I am still discovering deeper aspects of those things, after all this time and I know the process will not really end until i meet my heavenly father face to face. I wouldn't want it any other way. I fact, writing this book has been one more step on that journey for me.

I never thought I would tell my shame story, let alone share them in the chapters of a book. Those secrets held me back and kept me small. The weight of them was crushing. I spent most of my life guarding them and making sure no one really saw me.

The thing is, those stories demand to be told. The truth is nothing if not insistent. My secrets were making themselves known in toxic and harmful ways in my life – addiction, fear, Abuse, Human trafficking, control, rape, unhealthy relationships... All of those things were my story being told – I just wasn't the one telling it.

When I finally became unable, and eventually, unwilling, to keep those secrets anymore, I became a storyteller. By sharing my stories, by writing them down, by allowing myself to be seen in all my brokenness, I finally found healing and connection and joy.

What if the power to heal yourself has been yours all along? What if the secrets you've been carrying, those dark and heavy shame stories, are open to challenge? What would happen if you came to believe your stories are not unspeakable and you could survive the telling? What if you decided to tell the truth about your life story in order to write a new ending?

You can, you know.

Shame loses its Power when it is brought into the light and Out Of The Shadows.

ACKNOWLEDGMENTS

They say it takes a village to raise our children. Well, I've learned that it also takes one to write a memoir. There are so many people who have had such a huge impact on my life, Good and Bad, and the telling of my story. I want to extend so much love and appreciation to my fellow villagers who made this even possible for me to write this book.

My beautiful daughter Madison for being willing to read and edit the hardest parts of me. Some of these pages were filled with pain and I can only imagine what it must have felt like for her, but she wanted to be the one to do it. Without her, I couldn't have finished and fulfilled this dream. I am truly blessed to have her.

I don't even know the names of so many of the people who made a difference in my life back then. What I have learned is that kindness of others is this: Never underestimate the power of caring about someone else, making eye contact, Sharing a meal, a gentle smile, or touch. These simple meaningless gestures could mean the difference of someone taking their life or choosing to take their life back!

To all those unknown souls who smiled and me when I don't even think I existed, who hugged me when I needed it the most, and gave me help and support along the way; I thank each and every one of you from the bottom of my heart.

People from many walks of life have shown me grace throughout the years. These people did not pass judgment but rather, through their kindness, they gave me strength and hope when I had none. Each and every one of these people did or said something so profound, that it made it possible for me to be the person I am today. I love myself, I love who I have become!

Friendships have taken many forms as I have traveled my road to finding myself and healing that little girl inside of me. Many people have helped along the way, cared about me, and became my friends. Some appeared when life was still very much a mirage. There have been some great friendships with men too, along the way. These men showed me that all men are NOT the same, Not all men are Pimps and predators. I am grateful for these friendships. Art, Todd, Zane and Johnny, You all showed me that I can trust men. Your friendships healed a bitterness in me. Something my father and my abusers never did. I am forever in your debt xx

The telling of my story is so much stronger because of those who read my early drafts, stayed up late nights helping me process through memories, helping me let go of past pains that I had been holding onto for far too long, those who offered suggestions and feedback, You are all the real MVP's

As you finish this book, if you are a Survivor or maybe
you are someone who's ready to Level Up and Break
Free from your current situation. And I am here to tell
you, you can Sister!

This is what I declare over you:

Whatever rejection, fear or trauma that has been stolen
from you, I declare that the deepest desperation you've
experienced will lead you straight to God's greatest
revelation in your life.

I declare that the Lord will give you relief from your
unbelief. He will restore you, redeem you and write his
story- His glorious story onto the pages of your life.

Doubt, Fear and defeat have no place in the sacred sanctuary of your heart.

Bitterness, Resentment and anger have no place in a life as beautiful as yours.

From now on when misguided voices or the enemy himself tries to put you down with lies, pull you away from the truth or push you into anything that could derail your destiny, I pray that you will sense the mighty hand of the Lord.

You are destined for a life and a love that can never be diminished, tarnished, shaken or taken. We all have a story, You have a story!

First off, I want to start off by saying Thank You to each and every one of you that took the time to read my Memoir. For each and everyone of you, I am truly grateful. You have all given me the strength to continue "To Tell!", to bring my darkness "Out of the Shadows" and into the light.

It took me decades to even identify as a victim of Human Trafficking. Sadly, today, not all that much has really changed and there are still thousands and thousands of young children who are just like I was, out there being preyed upon, without even truly knowing they are even victims. They are raped, beaten, abused and traumatized by the people who are exploiting them and the men that seek to rent their bodies and steal parts of their soul. Ultimately sustaining the same trauma as war veterans. They carry their shame too for decades not understanding fully that they were or maybe still are, the victim. This is and continues to be the reality for countless victims right here in Canada.

It's the weak like this that has given me the motivation to take the leap and finally decide to write this book. Finally after decades of hiding my story from the world around me, I was giving myself a voice. I was giving them a voice. They are the reason I no longer keep my Shame hidden in the shadows and want to educate and advocate others in my community and around the country. We all really do have the power to make a difference in not just our own lives but the lives of everyone around us.

I'm going to share with you some key resources for both parents and young teens. I believe knowledge is the best tool. Knowing about this very real issue about Human Trafficking can make a huge difference in the prevention of our children being lured into the sex trade.

Parents Listen Up!!

Teach your children to arm yourselves with knowledge and so much self-love. Self-esteem is one of the best ways to ensure predators and pimps turn away. Remember they are targeting to those that are vulnerable and open to their manipulation and lies. I read once that a Pimp had told a vice officer, he would approach young girls and tell them they were beautiful. If the young girl looked down at the ground, he knew he could have her; the lack of self-esteem showed he could easily control her. However, if the young girl didn't look away and maintained eye contact, the pimp would leave her alone and move on to the next target.

Educate not just yourself but your children too. Human Trafficking is real and is happening right in our own communities and neighborhoods. Remember

Traffickers come in all ages, forms, and genders. Most young people who are trafficked will also recruit their peers.

For God's sake, In this day of social media, know where your kids are and what they are doing, especially online. Even though at times your teenager may seem distant and independent. We must remember they are still children who need our guidance, love and most of all advice without judgment. Take the time to learn about their world and how to stay connected.

If your child ever tells you that someone is hurting them or someone they know. Maybe someone has approached them and asked them to run away with them. If your child seems distant or depressed, or begins to act out or seems to be struggling, talk to them, take them to talk to someone.

Our Youth

Arm yourself with the highest self-esteem- Healthy self-love turns predators away.

Protect yourself with everything you have, especially online. If someone older than you approach you, befriends you and asks you to ever run away with them, they are not thinking about you at all, no matter how much you want to believe that they are. They are preying upon you and your weaknesses.

No matter how much pressure you ever feel, NEVER share nude photos, PERIOD! Those images are out there forever. Do not share your personal information and information about your family drama or fights with your parents. These predators troll the internet, looking for young people who seem unhappy at home and struggle with self-esteem. These people may seem like they are your friend and that they just "get you." But I'm here to tell you that they do not. They are lying to you. They say the same things to everyone who fits the description.

Join something. I don't care if it's a group or a team, whether its sports or a book club. Group settings, working together with your peers on goals is great for your self-worth and self-esteem.

Respect and value your own sexuality and body! Today we are surrounded by images of sex and scantily-clad women and girls are everywhere. Our young girls are being taught that being super sexy is what's needed and that having a boyfriend is the most important thing on the planet. I'm here to tell you, It is not, that is absolutely not true. First, we must learn to be happy and love ourselves. Our bodies belong to us and we really must value that. You can wait to have sex and No, means No!

This is to the young men; You don't have to prove you are a man by pressuring someone to have sex with you. Respect your girlfriend/boyfriend and yourself. It truly starts there!

Don't be afraid to ask your parents, teachers, councilors what human trafficking is. Learn about how and why it happens. Share what you learn with your peers. You are never to Young to make a difference, to change the course of your life or the life of someone else.

RESOURCES HERE IN CANADA

I Am Not 4 Sale app to help victims and report offenders

https://www.iamnotforsale.ca

Alliance Against Modern Slavery

http://www.allianceagainstmodernslavery.org

ACT Alberta

https://www.actalberta.org

Beyond Borders

http://www.beyondborders.org/en/home

Chrysalis Network & National Human Trafficking Support Line

http://www.chrysalisnetwork.org

Defend Dignity

https://defenddignity.ca

Free-Them

http://freethem.ca

Hope for the Sold

http://hopeforthesold.com

International Justice Mission Canada

https://www.ijm.ca

London Abused Women's Centre

https://www.lawc.on.ca

Ma Mawi Wi Chi Itata Centre

http://www.mamawi.com

Ottawa Coalition to End Human Trafficking

http://www.endhumantrafficking.ca

PACT Ottawa – Persons Against the Crime of

Trafficking in Humans

http://www.pact-ottawa.org

RCMP Human Trafficking National Coordination
Centre
http://www.rcmp-grc.gc.ca/ht-tp/index-eng.htm

REED – Resist Exploitation Embrace Dignity
http://embracedignity.org

Salvation Army Canada
https://salvationist.ca/action-support/human-trafficking

Sextrade 101
http://www.sextrade101.com

We Fight
http://wefight.ca

14692951R00126

Made in the USA
Middletown, DE
19 November 2018